Thanks for keeping Dems in-line and for keeping this book a secret. You Are a great singer

Thank You,

Tony Robbins

How Tony's success programs helped me design my life so *I can do what I want when I want*

◊

Manny Ibay, Esq.

destini books
santa monica, california

destini books

233 Wilshire Boulevard

4th Floor

Santa Monica, CA 90401

(310) 990-0217

First Destini Books Edition 2002

Manufactured in the United States of America

Library of Congress Control Number: 2002090111

ISBN 0-9717700-7-7

Cover & Layout by Crest Graphic Design

To my wife, Katie, as one of your wedding presents

To my parents, for your love and support

CONTENTS

INTRODUCTION

Some people believe that self-improvement books are a waste of their time. They also think they already know what it takes to succeed in all aspects of their lives. When they hear about a friend who "needs" to listen to someone like Tony Robbins, they assume this person must be weak. The truth is, if you aren't doing what you want when you want, you probably need some form of success coaching. Fortunately, there is plenty available in the form of books, tapes and live seminars. The purpose of this book is to show you the value of following a success program and how it has empowered me to design my dream life.

If you've watched any television in the past decade, you've probably seen Tony Robbins' infomercial about the best-selling self-improvement program of all time, *Personal Power*. In it, you've heard testimonials from such famous names as Andre Agassi, Pamela Anderson, and Leeza Gibbons. But you were probably wondering *how Tony's program could help the average Joe or Jane design his or her ideal life?* Something closer to your own aspirations. And you would have appreciated a detailed account of how someone used *Personal Power* in his daily life to accomplish this. What prompted him to start listening to that first tape? What obstacles did he face? What was he thinking and feeling throughout the process?

In this book you will read about someone whose starting place was probably even worse than yours. Someone who had *twenty-six* different jobs in his first seven years out of college. Someone who was earning only $1,000 per month when he started listening to *Personal Power*. Someone who actually got turned down for a job as a car salesman because of poor credit. Someone who had no idea of where his life was going and no excitement about the future.

This book will show how I was able to employ the life changing strategies in *Personal Power* to design a lifestyle that now allows me to do what I want when I want. A lifestyle that allowed me to take *thirty-six* vacations between 1995 and 2000. And most importantly, to create a life that now has purpose and excitement every single day.

You will read excerpts from my "success journal" that show the insights I gained in my ongoing pursuit of personal growth with Tony Robbins. I also discuss what you can learn from Tiger Woods and Michael Jordan, and how their beliefs parallel those of Tony Robbins. You will also discover how Tony helped his students following the crisis of "9-11" and how I employed his strategies at that point to reach an even higher level.

When I started out I didn't believe I needed to read anything on personal development and growth. I thought it was something I could figure out for myself. But I spent my first seven years after college floundering. I always thought I would join a big corporation in some entry-level position and become president within a couple of years, a plot very similar to *The Secret of My Success*, starring Michael J. Fox. Guess what? That only happens in the movies. While listening to Tony's infomercial, I wondered exactly how some of his students really made it. Average, underachieving people who started with almost nothing, not just celebrities like Andre Agassi and Leeza Gibbons who were already stars when they employed Tony. How could someone who started at rock bottom use Tony's strategies to design his ideal life?

This book began as a thank you letter to Tony that I started writing one day in my success journal. As it grew longer and longer, I began to realize that it could give others a valuable perspective on exactly how his system works in practice. I saw that various entries from my success journal might give readers an understanding of the transformation process. As you'll see, many of my most effective entries were simply answers to the questions that Tony posed in his daily assignments.

When I started, I had serious doubts as to whether I could be one of Tony's successful students. But I believed in Tony just enough to keep going and start applying what I had learned. Unfortunately, not everyone who purchases the *Personal Power* program listens to all of it. In fact, the person from whom I borrowed the tapes told me seven years later that she still had not finished listening to them. This book is dedicated to helping people like her – and maybe you – complete the journey.

I'm guessing that you may not be exactly where you want to be in your life. I was in the same position ten years ago. I had dug myself into such a hole that I considered my life lower than rock bottom. I wanted success, but had no idea of how to achieve it. Worse, I did not believe that I should have to work hard.

I assumed that I could be successful through a job that was not too stressful and did not require much hard work. That sounds pretty funny to me now. But I'll bet most people who don't have what they want have taken a similar attitude.

I stand as living proof that changing your attitude can change your life. By reading this book, in conjunction with Tony's best selling program *Personal Power*, you too will be able to design a life worth writing a book about. What I'm offering you here is a road map of how one underachiever used *Personal Power* to turn his life around.

Since I credit Tony with so much of what I have accomplished, I decided to include my thank you letter to him as the first chapter.

1

◆

THANK YOU, TONY!

Thank you, Tony Robbins! My initial encounter with your work was in 1991. Like millions of Americans, I first saw you on a late-night T.V. infomercial in which you advertised your *Personal Power* tapes. At the time, I was so broke I didn't even have a credit card to pay for the program. But I was able to borrow a set of your tapes from a friend, and took the thirty-day program seriously.

The results did not show up immediately. At the time, the best job I could get was selling long distance services in Los Angeles for $1,000/month plus commission. The sad part was that my monthly commissions never amounted to more than $300. Worse yet, I had to drive over forty-five miles each way to the company office, which was located near Disneyland. This was far from the life I had envisioned when I graduated from Case Western Reserve University. I was doing a job I found hateful and embarrassing – so much so that I avoided telling people what I did for a couple of years. I was so down on myself I actually cried when I thought about how far my life was from where I wanted it to be.

During my college years, I was an Alex P. Keaton fan (Michael J. Fox's character on *Family Ties*) and always envisioned myself as a big-time business guy, president of a major corporation and a world traveler, with all the finer things in life. But after several years of boring jobs that provided neither money, fame nor enough time to travel, I had almost resigned myself to living a life of mediocrity. Or as you put it, I was caught up in making a living instead of designing a life that I could be totally excited about and proud of.

I saw your infomercial several times before I actually got to listen to the tapes. By then, your message really grabbed me because I didn't think I had anything to lose, especially since I was able to borrow the tapes. (I have since bought most of your CD programs.) I thought my life was at rock bottom: no savings, no career, and – most devastatingly – no direction. As you have stated, most people do something either out of inspiration or desperation. For me it was out of desperation.

It's funny, but when I thought I was doing okay in life I saw these motivational courses offered on TV as just a bunch of BS. I didn't think they were something *I* would have any need for. And from my observation, there are many people out there who are so resigned to their life that they do nothing to change it. It was only when I felt so much pain that I needed to listen to what you had to say. What I have learned since then is that *everyone* – from the loser I used to be all the way up to Kobe Bryant – needs a coach to get him or her to the next level.

Most people remember you as the coach who took Andre Agassi from number thirty to number one in the span of six months. Or how you motivated Pamela Anderson to take action and reach superstardom in *Baywatch*. I wanted to write this book to show exactly how you can help an average person go from rock bottom to a life he could be totally excited about.

Let me give you a clearer picture of where I was before I listened to your tapes or read your books. I was living in a single apartment measuring about 450 square feet, with three dogs I acquired when I still had a functioning credit card. Although I didn't have to wash my dishes in the bathtub (we had a kitchenette), I didn't own a refrigerator for about a year and was living out of a Coleman picnic cooler that I refilled with ice every couple of days. I was driving a 1983 Volkswagon that I bought from one of those loan-shark car dealers in downtown Los Angeles because my credit was horrible – thanks to debts accumulated from pleasures long forgotten, trying to live large in Los Angeles without having the earning power to back me up. (With good credit the same monthly payment would have gotten me a BMW.)

But most painfully, I was working at a job that I hated. This job required me to drive all over Los Angeles – about 150 miles per day – trying to convince people to switch their long distance services. We all know how much we hate those calls from telemarketers late at night. But I had to do this face to face for a living. Imagine doing something you hated, something that you were embarrassed to tell anybody about, and making only about $1,300 per month doing it. (It netted only about $1,000 when I factored in the $300 per month spent in gas – and that was before taxes.)

And to think my parents had spent over $40,000 sending me to college to get a job like this. A life like this. I wasn't

uneducated or unskilled, but I was living day to day. There was
no money or time to travel, especially since I had already
exhausted all my credit resources. There was certainly no pride in
what I was doing. And the worst part was that I saw no way out
of this predicament. Thoughts about my destiny only depressed
me. I used to think my future was the California Super Lotto.
Every week I played, with the belief that this was my only
chance. The odds, of course, were equal to those of getting hit by
lightning.

At the time, I could not see any way to improve my situation.
College courses never taught us how to achieve success or how
to design a life that we could be excited about. All they taught us
was how to take tests and write papers. How I wish there had
been a *Personal Power* course at school. Even had I paid full
price for your course (approximately $179), it would have been
much cheaper than what my parents paid for just one credit hour
of college. (The average credit hour for most private universities
is about $400 to $500.) Your course taught me how to succeed in
life. Not just about making money, but how to manage and
control my mind so as to be happy and fulfilled. I always use
your power questions when I feel that I am not on track. It's
unbelievable how much good can come from asking oneself:
"What is great in my life right now?" and making a list of the
answers.

When I first started listening to your tapes I would play them
in a portable tape player in my Volkswagon (my car was totally
devoid of audio components) while driving around Los Angeles
between sales appointments. I did the exercises religiously
because I sensed this was my only hope for success. I was so
"gung ho" that I even listened to the tapes when I had to bring a

sales trainee around for the day. When he began questioning my interest, I defended them as though they were gospel. And I'm glad now that I did.

The results did not come immediately. And my goals have changed and evolved since I first listened to your tapes. But the best part about my life right now is that I am equally excited about every day – whether it be a Monday or a Friday – and I get charged up when I think about my future.

Since starting your tape program in early 1992, I have come a long way. The first thing I did was to get happy about where I currently was in life. I strongly believe in your statement that we need to happily achieve instead of achieve to be happy. I think that was part of my problem. I was always thinking that I would be happy after I got my Mercedes or my house in Bel Air. Instead, you advocate using power questions to put us in the right state to reach our potential. I started each day using your morning power questions: "What fun things can I do today while I am at work? What is great in my life right now?" This enabled me to get into a powerful state. It certainly was better than waking up and asking myself, "Why do I have to go to this crappy job today?"

Now, whenever a friend is depressed or in a rut, the first thing I ask him or her is: "What are you excited about – or what could you be excited about – right now? A good friend of mine was having problems with his wife and felt pessimistic about working them out. He seemed reluctant to try anything and was about to give up. You know how it is. People get frustrated and all they focus on is what is wrong with their spouse. Since I was the best man at their wedding, I really wanted to see their relationship work out, and I consider what I did to help them very Tony Robbins-esque. I knew from talking to both of them that most of their problems were little things. This is what I said: "I will send you a check for $50 today if you sit down together and write ten things you really love about your spouse and fax this list to me tonight by 9 p.m." Fortunately, they were just starting out and needed the money, so they faxed me their lists by that evening, and I sent them the $50. And by golly, things improved. They started to focus on what was great about each other instead of the petty little things: "You don't take care of the baby enough." "You don't put your clothes away."

Getting back to my own story, I used that same positive energy to plan my dream life, no matter how unrealistic it sounded at the time. I loved the goal-setting workshop where you give your listeners a chance to write down everything they want, as though they were a kid on Christmas Eve sitting in Santa's lap. Boy, did I have a big list! The next thing you do is ask us to write down why we want each of these goals – The Power of Why. This really got my juices flowing and showed me the reasons I wanted these things on my list. Naturally, I didn't pursue everything I wrote down because your question, "Why do I want these goals?" also weeded out the ones I wasn't seriously committed to.

The two goals I took seriously were:

1) *To have my own business where I can do what I want when I want.*

   One thing I truly believe is that success is not only about the money. You can have plenty of cash in your bank account, but if you are not doing what you want, you will always be unsatisfied.

2) *To be able to travel as frequently as possible.*

   I discovered earlier in my life that the thing that got

me most excited was going on a trip to a new destination. Luckily, I was able to finance a couple of nice vacations before the money ran out. Just the thought of going on a trip in the near future got me to work harder. People have to figure out what they really want if they are to perform at their best level.

After listening to your tapes and determining what I wanted, I was able to focus all my energy and time on reaching these goals. But this was by no means easy. There were times when I thought it was impossible to reach these goals. Especially since I was making less than $1,000 per month after taxes. The key was to put myself in a position to be able to reach these goals.

As I am about to list some of my accomplishments, I can feel a chill of excitement running down my spine at telling you where I was able to travel during a short period of time. Between April 1995 and June 2000, these are the cities I visited on what I called the Manny Ibay World Tour:

1)	April 1995	New York, NY
2)	May 1995	Monterey, CA
3)	June 1995	Long Island, NY
4)	July 1995	Ft. Lauderdale, FL
5)	August 1995	London, England
		Paris, France
		Cannes, France
		Monte Carlo, Monaco
		Venice, Italy
		Rome, Italy
6)	October 1995	New York, NY
		Cleveland, OH (during World Series)

7)	December 1995	Manila/Iloilo, Philippines
8)	February 1996	San Francisco, CA
9)	March 1996	Miami, FL
10)	May 1996	San Francisco, CA
11)	August 1996	Waikiki Beach, HI
12)	September 1996	Madison, WI
13)	October 1996	Washington, D.C.
14)	November 1996	Las Vegas, NV
15)	December 1996	Manila/Iloilo, Philippines
16)	January 1997	Ft. Lauderdale, FL
		Key West, FL
		Orlando, FL
17)	March 1997	Las Vegas, NV
18)	May 1997	Sydney, Australia
19)	July 1997	Las Vegas, NV
20)	October 1997	Madison, WI
21)	December 1997	Manila/Iloilo, Philippines
22)	March 1998	Las Vegas, NV
23)	April 1998	Maui, HI
24)	August 1998	Maui, HI
		Waikiki Beach, HI
25)	September 1998	Vancouver, British Columbia, Canada
26)	November 1998	Carmel, CA
27)	December 1998	Niagara Falls, NY
		Rochester, NY
28)	January 1999	Maui, HI
29)	April 1999	Santa Barbara, CA
30)	May 1999	London, England
		Paris, France

	Marseilles, France
	Florence, Italy
31) July 1999	Sonoma, CA
	San Francisco, CA
32) November 1999	Las Vegas, NV
33) December 1999	Buffalo, NY
34) February 2000	La Jolla, CA
35) May 1999	Santa Barbara, CA
36) June 2000	Ft. Lauderdale, FL
	Nassau, Bahamas
	St. Thomas/St. John, Virgin Islands
	San Juan, Puerto Rico

I am extremely proud of all the traveling I did. When I started *Personal Power* I could never have imagined taking thirty-six vacations in five years. That is more trips than many people take in a lifetime. Remember, I had not traveled for over two years when I began your program. Traveling as much as possible is one of the goals I set in your goal-setting workshop. As you say in *Personal Power*, "I'm not telling this to impress you, but to impress upon you the power of having definite goals in my life." The best part is that all those vacations did not cost anywhere near the amount one would imagine. Many times I got to stay with friends or relatives. I was also lucky enough to have my parents and brother sponsor a few of those trips. The key was to make abundant travel a major goal, one that I had committed to paper, with plenty of reasons for wanting it. Once I did so, opportunities appeared from every direction.

I probably didn't save as much money as I could have or should have. But that was not my goal at the time. More importantly, the confidence I gained from accomplishing a major goal has energized and enabled me to make more money in my current business endeavors. Did you ever notice that you become more dedicated and efficient when you know what you are working for?

As you can see from my list, my traveling slowed down in 2000. And this was no accident. I consciously decided to modify my goals, focusing primarily on increasing my business since I was planning to get married in 2001. By now you are probably wondering what I was doing for a living, traveling like a jet-setter. Which brings me to the best part of my story. Shortly after listening to the *Personal Power* audiotapes and reading *Awaken the Giant Within*, I decided to take control of my destiny and design a life that I could be excited about. I realized that I could never be happy in a corporate setting because it did not offer me the time flexibility to be able to travel frequently. I would have to start my own business.

This was the most difficult part of the process for me, as it is bound to be for anyone who needs to make such a change. But the most important thing was that I knew, in order to have the lifestyle I craved, I needed to find a business I could create that would enable me to control my work schedule and make my own rules. In the meantime, I still needed to pay for rent, food and other necessities. For the next ten months, I continued to perform a variety of jobs, including selling vending machines and telemarketing. They provided enough to pay the rent, but not much more. However, for the first time in a long while, I was able to enjoy myself, knowing that I had a long-term goal beyond merely paying my bills. So each day I would go to work, but always foremost in my thinking was my determination to design a life that would enable me to do the things I dreamed about.

Many ideas ran through my head. I thought about becoming a real estate broker, operating a property management company, owning/supplying vending machines, running a messenger service, and management consulting. After giving each of these ideas serious consideration I decided they were not for me. But I was actively searching, open to possibilities. I saw my current job as a temporary stepping-stone to brighter days.

It was not until New Year's Eve, 1992 that I finally began to envision my future clearly. I met my parents in Las Vegas for the holiday and we were talking during a late-night dinner. They knew I was not happy with the jobs I had been doing for the past year. But they also knew that I had been reluctant to discuss the subject in the past. Fortunately, the *Personal Power* tapes taught me to how to break through my fears. The program enabled me to discuss my future frankly, and I invited my parents to make recommendations.

They suggested that I think again about going to law school. I had already considered the law two years earlier, but gave it up after the first two weeks of studying for the LSAT. My initial reaction to my parents' idea was negative. I didn't think I could get motivated to study again, remembering my earlier failure.

I had vivid memories of that first attempt: driving to the Pepperdine University School of Law library sometime in 1990 to study for the LSAT. I recalled taking the practice exam in the guidebook and doing abysmally. On one of my many breaks I walked through the library and looked at all those thick legal books. Even if I managed to get into law school, I'd still have all these books to read. Impossible to proceed in the face of such a task, my dream of going to law school died a few weeks later. For the next year, I kept telling myself that I couldn't have made it anyway. But that was in 1990, before I listened to *Personal Power*.

Even after hearing your tapes, I did not immediately decide to go back to school. I told my parents I appreciated their help and would consider their recommendation for the next few weeks since I had until February 14, 1993 to take the LSAT. I returned home to Los Angeles and resumed my job as sales rep for a company that leased vending machines.

After about a week, I called my parents and told them I had decided to take their suggestion about law school. Initially, I believe it was a knee-jerk reaction because I so hated going back to that job. But in time – especially when I needed to study in the wee hours of the night (after working all day selling vending equipment) – it was my desire to have the type of life you talk about in your tapes that kept me going this time around.

Once I got over that hurdle and got accepted into Pepperdine University School of Law, things became easier. My goal of having my own business was coming into focus. It was no longer a dream on a piece of paper, but reality taking shape before my eyes.

Contrary to most of the people in my class who aspired to work at a big, prestigious firm, à la Tom Cruise in *The Firm*, I always knew I wanted my own practice so I could have the freedom to travel frequently and set my own schedule. And I believe that knowing this from Day One helped when the time came for me to go out and start cultivating a business.

I credit you with helping me get to where I am today. Even though I'm not a multi-millionaire or super famous, I am doing what I want when I want every day. In addition, I am able to enjoy the finer things of life – plenty of travel, a Mercedes-Benz SL500 convertible, a beautiful place to live, dinners at Spago and Kenneth Cole shoes. The best part is that I now have the ability to control my destiny. I decide what I will do tomorrow, whether it be going to the office to work super hard for my clients, playing golf, taking a trip to Hawaii, or just taking a Ferris Bueller's Day Off with no need to pretend I'm sick.

I cannot begin to tell you what a liberating feeling it is to know that I alone decide what I will do when I wake up in the morning. I can honestly say that *Personal Power* helped me design a life I can be excited about each and every day. And for me that is the most important message you have to offer.

I'd like to give you a question to ask at your next seminar that will help your students figure out whether they are doing what they want in life. Ask them: "Are you as excited about getting out of bed on a Monday as you are on a Saturday?"

Thanks to you, I know that I am. And I'm sure many of today's greatest successes will tell you the same thing.

2

---◆---

GETTING STARTED

Tony says that only 10 percent of the people who buy a book ever read past the first chapter. So you must be in that top 10 percent. The goal now is to get you in the top half of one percent who are living a life they are excited about and proud of.

Remember, the goal of this book and all of Tony's work is to help you design your life, as you would like it to be. Not like mine, Tony's, or your parents', but *yours*. By reading my journey through *Personal Power* you will see the benefits of a success program for making your own dream come true.

I am a lawyer by trade. I do not make a living from giving personal peak performance seminars or writing books. Like most of you, I saw Tony Robbins for the first time on a late night infomercial. I had seen other ads for money-making schemes in real estate and government auctions, but nothing that was seriously geared toward designing a new life for myself. Even at first glance, *Personal Power* looked appealing. I probably watched the infomercial another ten times just for the motivation and excitement it provided. (Of course, later on I watched it just to see Pamela Anderson!) Fortunately, a friend let me borrow the *Personal Power* program. Since I had to return the tapes in the near future, I got to work immediately.

The best part about the tapes (there were no CD's back then) is that Tony speaks with an incredible level of energy. He really makes you want to leap out of your chair and start designing your life *now*. And believe me, I needed that kind of energizing. When I started the tape program, I was in a state of mental despair. I may have been doing slightly better than Tony did at the beginning. He was living in a 400 square-foot bachelor apartment in Venice, CA, washing his dishes in the bathtub, thirty-eight pounds overweight, alone, broke and frustrated. At least I was not overweight or alone!

I actually started the program on New Year's Day, 1992. It was one of my resolutions. If you can, I highly recommend that you start *Personal Power* (it has been improved and revised to *Personal Power 2*) on some significant day, e.g., your 40th birthday, the day after you are laid off, the day you decide to start losing weight.

The most memorable thing about that New Year was that I had to work on the day of New Year's Eve. The company I worked for told us we were not going to get that day off. I remember begging our supervisor for the time off: "Who in their right mind is thinking of changing their long distance service today?"

And, in fact, that was the last year I ever worked between December 23 and January 1. I am a big fan of Christmas. I believe it is a time to celebrate with your loved ones, enjoy the fruits of your hard work and give lots of nice presents (as well as getting some). Now, I'm not opposed to anyone working on those days – as long as that is something you want to do.

Taking Control of My Destiny

Obviously, there was a lot of pent up frustration in me when I started Tony's program. I really hated working on December 31st. I remember saying then that I wanted to design my life so I would never have to work on December 31st again.

When I was listening to the *Personal Power* audiocassettes for the first time during that period, I thought it was the best program I have ever heard, for learning how to take control of my mind and my life. This was no get-rich-quick scheme. Not some hyperactive guy telling me how to become a millionaire by placing small ads in local papers. Nor was it an Asian gentlemen standing on a yacht with several busty women in bikinis, telling me how I could make money in real estate. Tony simply showed me how I could tap into my *Personal Power*.

This is not an overnight success program. By following it, you can achieve a lot in the first couple of days, in terms of improving your psychology, but don't expect it to make you rich (in dollar terms) right away. And if money is not your goal, it never will. You are better off knowing that up front, if you are going to make real strides in your personal development.

You may have seen Jeff Arch, in Tony's infomercial, telling how he wrote *Sleepless in Seattle* immediately after attending Tony's seminar. A true story, but more likely the exception than the rule. *Personal Power* teaches you how to design an ideal life – without necessarily hitting the jackpot immediately. That would be nice, but it's not something you should rely on.

Creating a Realistic Timeline

What you should count on is that it will take some time and effort to get to your ideal lifestyle. Naturally, the bigger goals your goals, the longer the process will take. If you want to be the next Bill Gates or Tiger Woods, getting there will probably take you at least as long as it took them. (Remember, Tiger has been playing golf since he was six months old!) However, if your goal is to lose thirty pounds, that may be possible in thirty days, as Tony has shown. What everyone out there needs to realize is that there is no such thing as an unrealistic goal. There are only unrealistic timelines for reaching those goals.

If you were working for $1,000 per month selling long distance services and you told me that your goal was to be a millionaire in six months, (without doing anything else or winning the lottery), I would consider you unrealistic. However, if you told me that your goal was to be a millionaire in six months and that you had developed a success conditioning tape program that you would actively market using infomercials and if you also told me that you were spending over 200 days a year on the road giving seminars to thousands of people at a time, then I would think you had a realistic goal. And that is how Tony got to be a millionaire in less than six months. *Dream big*, but also have a plan. Don't base your dream of the future on the lottery.

The more I listened to *Personal Power*, the more my attitude changed to taking responsibility for my plight. I no longer tried to blame others for my failures. I realized I was in that predicament because of *me*!

I know there are exceptions to this rule. Some people are in tough situations through no fault of their own. However, many of us have dug ourselves into whatever hole we are currently in. I personally was unable to repay all the debt I had accumulated immediately after college. I kept thinking that my income would increase and that I would easily be able to pay off the credit cards. But guess what? That did not happen. When you are continually changing jobs, your income does not go up. You are lucky if it stays the same. But all that time in between is what destroys any chance you might have of staying ahead of your creditors.

Developing a Framework for Success

Once I realized that I alone was responsible for my own life, I decided to get serious. I really immersed myself in Tony's tape program, his book *Awaken the Giant Within*, and any other success books I could get my hands on. I remember Tony saying, "If you want success, you've got to study it." But this is something I was never taught in school, nor were most people I know. If you haven't studied success in the past, you need to start now. Use this book as a springboard to many others.

If you have not already read Tony's *Awaken the Giant Within*, I urge you to get it as soon as possible. It is like an operating manual for your mind that will make you function at a more efficient and productive level. Between Tony's tapes and his book, I finally developed a framework for success in my thinking.

For the first thirty days I listened to the *Personal Power* program. It was easy for me to listen to the tapes because I spent at least three to four hours driving per day while I was selling long distance services. I did all the exercises at the end of each session between sales calls and when I got home. It became something I really looked forward to doing when I got up in the morning because I felt that I was on to something important. I felt I had an opportunity to start my life all over again.

Tony can make you forget about your terrible or mediocre past and move forward. I started to believe that as long as I followed what he said, I was going to succeed. At the time, I was not reading any other material, just focusing on what Tony had to say. I think when you are starting out, it is best to hear only one voice because that way there are no contradictions to discourage you. Only after you have some momentum on your way to success do I recommend reviewing other writers' work.

As I write this book, a decade from when I started listening to Tony's tapes, my dream life has become a reality. A couple of months ago I had dinner with the person who let me borrow the *Personal Power* tapes. I had not seen her in about seven years and we were catching up about what had been happening in our lives. After I told her about all my traveling and the business I was now running, she said,

"Wow! Those tapes really did work!"

3

---◆---

SEEING CHANGES

Immediately after completing Tony's 30-day program, I noticed that my thinking had shifted from how to survive to how to succeed. Before starting the program I was focused on paying my bills, deciding what to watch on TV, and looking forward to the weekend. Like most people, I wanted a better job and a better life, but never took any real action to achieve it. I did not know how. After the initial thirty days of *Personal Power*, things started to change.

Keeping a Success Journal

I think the best new habit I developed was to keep a success journal as Tony highly recommends. It was not something I started on Day One, but I did begin to write in it regularly when I started reading *Awaken the Giant Within*. Initially, I used it just to take notes, but it evolved quickly into a place where I wrote down my goals and what I needed to do to accomplish them. It really fueled the fire of my ambition to design *my* ideal life. Writing your goals down on paper and reviewing them often helps to transform them from dreams to reality.

During that first year, I managed to write something almost every day. On the first few pages of my success journal I wrote:

1992

Decided that learning about success will be my #1 priority, which translates to reading every day, one book per month, and taking the necessary action to apply what I have learned. Decided to take control of my destiny. I have to work hard so I won't be in a position where I am not in control. Use this as a motivating force to keep you on your road toward success. I realized that all the failures of my past are what is going to make me a tremendous success in the future. I can feel the motivation flowing through me. I know that major success is on the horizon. Just be sure to handle temporary failure – like not getting any sales in the beginning – as simply that, temporary.

I must see past the short term and focus on my long-term goals so that I will have everything I want. Nothing can stop me except me. I think I know how to handle failure so it will never stop me again. Use the past two months and 40+ interviews as a reference toward the relation of massive failure = success.

Always use references when you begin to doubt a belief. If I question that I am a great salesman, refer back to the reasons why I believe I am. Always seek positive references. Constantly remind yourself when you are bored to do something productive. Remember, work hard, play hard.

I wrote all of that within months of listening to Tony's tapes. (And that was copied word for word, directly from my journal.) I sounded pretty motivated back then, didn't I? But at the time, as you can gather, I was unemployed and looking for a new job. It is amazing what your mind can do when you start committing all of your ideas and goals to paper.

Since then I have been a strong believer in that process. Although I did not keep great journals when I was in law school (I really did study), I have been a fanatic about it during the last four years and have a beautiful row of success journals in a bookcase in my bedroom. (I have since renamed them Superman Success Journals – since I am using a journal that has a Superman emblem on the front cover and every page. Hey, you've got to do everything possible to get yourself motivated to the highest level.)

At first, my journal consisted mostly of information that I copied from Tony's book. But soon I began incorporating material that I read or listened to and translated it into something that would motivate me to take action. It has also been a place to find solutions for my problems. During those moments when I am not totally focused or feeling too happy, I open my success journal and write on the top of a page:

What is great in my life right now?

Then I sit there and seriously think about the answers. It really works. My Superman Success Journals (SSJ) can look repetitious. At times, I wrote down my goals in life three times in one week. At other times I asked, "What is great in my life?" three days in a row. But that is the key. You've got to do whatever it takes to pump yourself up. And as Tony says, this is not merely "positive thinking." If you answer these questions seriously you have *real* reasons for being happy.

Let me give you another excerpt from my SSJ. I had just started a new job working as a sales rep for a vending machine company. It was not my dream job by any means, but at the time I needed a job to survive. Instead of seeing it as the dead-end job it might have been, I instead wrote the following in my SSJ:

What is great about working as a sales rep for ADV?

1)   Working as a sales rep is something that I am good at.
2)   Flexible schedule – I only need to go to the office when necessary.
3)   The management staff is excellent and they really like me.
4)   I can spend time on my success journal &
      studying between sales leads to get me pumped up.
5)   No required cold-calling. Only if I feel like it.
6)   Other reps earning $4 – $6K per month after a few months.
7)   Getting $1,750/mo. salary!

I made that job sound amazing. And at the time, it really was for me. (I had just left a job that paid only $1,000 per month.) You may be thinking, This does not seem like such a great life. However, before you can consider starting your own business and traveling around the world, you must pay your rent and put food on the table. Back then, I was barely at that level.

But it does take time for most people to make major strides. And the sooner you realize that, the closer you will be to achieving your dream life. One thing Tony mentions in his book is that people overestimate what they can accomplish in a year and underestimate what they can accomplish in a decade.

Although I was making only $1,750 per month working for someone else, I did have one major thing going for me during the first few months post *Personal Power*. I started to think and sound (at least in my journal) like someone successful. You have to start there before anything can happen to get you to your success goals. Only after you have the basic necessities in life can you start thinking about getting ahead. If you don't have food and shelter, you must spend all your time focusing on how to get them. But once the basics become a given, your mind will start looking to improve your situation.

Setting Clear Goals

Now that I had reached a level of subsistence, I began to think about what goals I really wanted in the future:

1992
Goals:
1) *Make $100k as a sales manager for San Fernando Valley office.*
2) *Cruise to my last job in a BMW convertible and show them that I am not a loser.*
3) *One week in St. Thomas by end of the year.*

4) *Complete Tony Robbins book by July 5.*
5) *Start new book July 6.*
6) *Continue weight lifting program.*
7) *Continue success journal.*
8) *Be #1 in office after 3 months.*
9) *Think for 15 minutes per day about how to make more money and be in control of my own destiny.*

Although I was still working like a dog for someone else, the genesis of my future dream life was beginning on paper. Not all of those goals were accomplished. I never became a sales manager because I decided that I did not want to work for someone else and be limited to two weeks of vacation per year. I did get a BMW sometime later. I did spend one week in Montego Bay, Jamaica instead of the Virgin Islands. (I finally got to the Virgin Islands last year.) I completed the Tony Robbins book in July (and have read it at least 10 times since). I did start reading another success book. I am still lifting weights. I am still doing my success journal. And I really did think about how to make more money and take control of my destiny. That is why I am here writing about it today.

After a short time I started thinking that I could be a success consultant. When I heard a friend describe his problems, I would immediately quote some technique I learned in the tapes to help resolve them. This success mentality becomes contagious after a couple of tapes. No matter how small the results seem, it's important to keep going. At least to maintain the success mind-set that Tony talks about for the 30 days.

4

---◆---

CREATING AN
EXCITING FUTURE

My favorite chapter in Tony's book is the one devoted to creating a compelling future. It's the one I always read when I feel I am off course or need an extra boost. In it, Tony talks about the power of goal setting and the importance of understanding why you want those goals. This was really the starting point for where I am today. Prior to reading his book and listening to the tapes, I was obviously not excited about my place in life. Whenever I compared my life to the lives of more successful people, I always got down on myself. It almost seemed as though I wasn't meant to have the type of life I saw others enjoying. I hated seeing people driving in fancy cars. And believe me, in Los Angeles you see a Ferrari, Porsche or Mercedes every ten seconds while driving down many streets.

I hated driving through Beverly Hills or Bel Air, seeing all the amazing houses I thought I would never own or even get a chance to live in. And it was painful going to the Beverly Center shopping mall to see all the exquisite designer clothes – Giorgio

Armani, Hugo Boss and Calvin Klein have always been my favorites. And of course, Kenneth Cole shoes. These luxuries were well beyond what I could afford. A Hugo Boss suit would have cost me more than a month's rent in those days.

I must say that living in Los Angeles, especially on the west side (Beverly Hills, Santa Monica, Bel Air, Brentwood, and Westwood) is uncomfortable for someone who wants all the finer things in life but can't afford them. You notice that many people seem to do nothing for a living except go out and shop, eat at outdoor cafes on Sunset Boulevard, or sip their café mochas at the Coffee Bean. I was always wondering how they have the time or money to do such things. Would it be better to live in a city like Cleveland or Detroit where there were a lot more "regular Joes"? But I loved the idea that the temperature could be 80 degrees in January when the rest of the country was under a foot of snow.

I never gave any serious consideration to moving since I believe Los Angeles is the best place in the world to live – as long as you can afford it. The point I want to make is that when you are trying to design your ideal life, you must first decide if you are living where you really want to. If you are not happy with your city, then you can't claim to have designed the ideal lifestyle for yourself. I don't think I truly realized Los Angeles was *my* city until I started traveling around the world. I was always pumped up when we landed at LAX regardless of whether I'd been to Paris or Maui. I never was excited to get back home from a great vacation when I lived in Cleveland or Long Island, NY. Now I'm not suggesting that everyone who reads this should sell their house and move to California, but if you are one of those people who say you hate where you live – and there are many people here who hate Los Angeles – I say *get out*!

Okay, so at least I was happy about where I was living. But I was unhappy about almost everything else which, in retrospect, was a good thing. If I'd been content with my lot in life, as many people are (either from having little ambition or from fear of failing) I might have lived that mediocre existence of working Monday through Friday, 9 to 5, just to make enough money to pay my bills and have modest entertainment. Of course, not everyone needs to have their own business. There are many people out there who have great jobs they enjoy doing (most of the time), jobs that offer the possibility of making a lot of money. But I neither liked what I was doing nor found the pay sufficient. You need at least one of those things to keep going. I'm sure many people would accept a lower salary if their job involved playing golf every day.

I needed to do something about my situation and fast. Thank God for the *Personal Power* program.

Writing Down Your Dreams

Tony's goal setting workshop started me thinking about my long-term future. Rather than merely mulling over what I might do the following weekend with my mediocre paycheck, I started to focus on what I wanted for the next ten or twenty years. Tony gets you to write down everything you want in life in several categories:

1) Personal development
2) Career/economic
3) Toys/adventure
4) Contribution

I have done this exercise many times over the past ten years. One thing you will notice on the road to your ideal life is that your goals keep changing. Some of the things I wanted five years ago are totally different than what I want today. Here is what I wrote down in 1992:

Personal Development Goals
1) *Master the material from Tony Robbins*
2) *Work out 3x/week for next 12 months and have super hot body*
3) *Read one book per month*
4) *Write success articles for Dante's newspaper*

Career/Business/Economic Goals
1) *Make $100k as sales manager*
2) *Start my own business within three years*
3) *Continue to "work" as much as I want until I decide to retire*
4) *Control my own destiny*

Toys/Adventure Goals
1) *House on the beach in Malibu*
2) *BMW convertible*
3) *Mercedes Benz S-class*
4) *4 weeks per year in Hawaii*
5) *4 weeks per year traveling to new places such as, Europe, Australia, Asia, Caribbean*
6) *GQ success wardrobe & cool fun clothes*
7) *Ability to sing with a band whenever I want*
8) *Go to all the big time events – Superbowl, US Open, Duran Duran*

9) *Get a refrigerator and all home appliances for house*
10) *Great workout room with weights*
11) *Get a computer to work on my book*

Contribution Goals
1) *After I have made it big, write a book on my life and success that will explain to the average guy what it takes.*
2) *Do seminars with Tony Robbins and assist others to make their life as good as mine*
3) *Teach class of college students about success*
4) *Write monthly success articles*

It is exciting to read what I wrote ten years ago. Some of these things I accomplished and others I never pursued. However, the ones I did achieve all started as ideas written down on paper. As I said, one of the best things I learned from Tony was to keep a success journal. It is continually invigorating to see how far you have come. Even in the beginning, when I was not making major strides, little things such as handling a crisis, working out for five straight days, or having the confidence to talk to that pretty girl in the elevator, felt good to read about. Reading my success journal was especially helpful on days when I thought I was not making progress toward anything. One big change in myself I've become aware of through rereading my journals: I no longer compare myself to other people – something I used to do all the time. Now I compare myself to how far I have improved since the last success journal.

That was Then, This is Now

Although my achievements may not seem like *mega* accomplishments when compared to a Bill Gates, a Tiger Woods or a Tony Robbins, these are the ones I am most excited about because they illustrate my development during the past ten years (when compared to my goals and situation in 1992):

1) I am in control of my own destiny. I decide how much I want to work, when to go to the office and when to go on vacation.

   (Previously, someone else always controlled my destiny. I was limited to two weeks of vacation per year.)

2) I have my own business – first as a paralegal and now as an attorney for the past five years. The business is generating enough money so that I can do what I want when I want.

   (Previously, I was always working for someone else. Someone was always there to tell me what I should or shouldn't do. I was earning only $1,000 per month.)

3) I have been running and lifting weights regularly for the past seven years.

   (Previously, I never worked out for more than a couple weeks at a time and never did any running except when it was required in school.)

4) I have done extensive traveling. In fact, I went on 36 separate vacations from April 1995 to June 2000. That's over seven per year!

(Previously I went on zero vacations from September 1990 to November 1992.)

5) I have learned a great deal of information about the field of personal development. During the past several years, I have read about one success-oriented book every two months.

(Previously, I never read success books. Most of my time was spent reading fiction.)

6) I am driving a BMW 525i and a Mercedes SL 500 convertible.

(Previously, I was driving a 1983 Volkswagon.)

7) I own a great place in a desirable part of town.

(Previously, I was living in a 450-square-foot single rented apartment. My credit was so bad that I couldn't even sign the lease myself. I needed a friend to sneak me into the place using his name – thanks, Ron!)

Dreaming Big

One last, but crucial point regarding "goal setting." Don't dream conservatively. When you are thinking about a dream home that you plan to purchase five years from now, don't start skimping on what you really want. If you are going to dream, dream big. For instance, if you want to have a seven-bedroom, nine-and-one-half-bath mansion, don't start by skimping on your location. Don't say to yourself, "Well, if I moved to this less desirable area, I could get it for a lot less." That will only sap your level of desire and motivation. The purpose of a big goal is to get you pumped up. Could you honestly get super excited if you were planning to get that mansion in an undesirable part of town? Don't be "realistic" about what you plan to accomplish five or ten years from now.

I'm not saying that you should spend your money foolishly. Five years from now you may weigh your desires and financial situation and determine that you have to sacrifice a little on location or on the number of bedrooms. But that is just being smart. When the time comes for you to plunk the money down on a house (or whatever) it will be perfectly okay to skimp on certain items based on your budget. When the future arrives, it will be all right to be "realistic." But not while you are dreaming about your goals five years before you are supposed to reach them. *Dreaming big* is the best way to get you to take massive action.

Let's look at a great example. I'm guessing that Kobe Bryant wants to be the greatest basketball player of all time. He wants to be better than Michael. He has wanted that since he came to the NBA. You might have said back then that he was being unrealistic, that he should probably just try to be a *good* player, rather than the *greatest* player. Fortunately for the NBA, he aspires to be the best ever. Do you think that someone who just won the NBA championship at 21 years of age (and was making tons of money) would be motivated to work super hard on his game during the off-season, if his goal was merely be a *good* player? Most people with lesser goals would just have partied the summer away. It is this "ridiculous" goal that motivates Kobe to keep working harder to improve. We should all have such "ridiculous" goals.

I remember when I was making $1,000 per month and dreaming about driving a Mercedes or a Ferrari. Back then, I didn't talk about it with my friends or family because I would have sounded crazy. I figured they would be thinking, How is this loser, who makes $1,000 per month going to drive such a car? Well, I dreamed really big for someone making so little money. But my "ridiculous" goal motivated me to really work hard and focus on what I could do, in order to afford such a luxury. Had I been realistic and thought only of something I could afford at the time, I doubt I would have put in the same effort. It is possible that you won't be able to get every single thing you want in five years. That's okay, I certainly haven't. Even Tony didn't accomplish every goal he wrote down on the back of that Russian map (the place where Tony wrote down his initial goals).

Walking Your Talk

Within three months of listening to *Personal Power*, I already was starting to think like Tony. I wrote the following article about goal setting despite the fact that I was still living in a 450-square-foot single apartment and making only $1,000 per month. I decided to include this article here to show you that it is never too early to start thinking that you could be the next Tony Robbins/Kobe Bryant/Bill Gates.

(Reprinted from *La Nacion*, a bilingual newspaper serving the Hispanic community, published by Viscarra Communications in 1992.)

How about goals in your life?

By Manny Ibay

Do you remember the last time you went grocery shopping without a list? I'll bet it was a nightmare. You had an idea of what you wanted, but without having planned ahead, you found yourself pushing your cart up and down the same aisles, trying to determine your needs as you went along. And when you got home, you noticed that there were several items that were completely forgotten. However, if you had started with a well thought-out list (something which takes only a few minutes to prepare), your trip would most assuredly have been successful the first time.

By the same token, one wonders why it is that so few of us have a list of goals which we want to accomplish in life? A well-known study at Yale University, some thirty years ago, found that a mere three percent of the graduating class had well thought-out written goals. Twenty years later, a follow-up study found that the same three percent outperformed (in financial terms) the other ninety-seven combined. That is the power of written goals.

Obviously, a list of goals is not the only requirement for realizing success. It is, however, the place to start. If you want to achieve and succeed in life, start by writing down your hopes and aspirations on a piece of paper. Follow up by actively pursuing avenues to making those written goals a reality.

It makes a great difference when you can add feelings of excitement and enthusiasm to what initially began as a sketchy and unrefined concept in your mind. Go out and look for opportunities which are related to that which you are interested in. You will soon be snowballing with ideas for achievement.

The choice is yours. Would you rather spend ludicrous amounts of time in the "grocery store of life," without a list, moving from job to job with no real future in sight? Or, would you prefer to take a minimal amount of time to write down and focus on what it is you want to do with your life? The choice is obvious.

I wrote this article just a few short months after completing the *Personal Power* program. Start acting like a successful individual and you will eventually grow into the person you want to become. You need the mindset first, before you start to see any kind of material accomplishments. Don't feel that it is ever too soon for you to start acting successful. It will really motivate you to walk your talk.

◆ Making a Start ◆

I challenge you to write down your own goals using Tony's categories on the next few pages. Do you want to be in the top 3 percent or bottom 97 percent? Is there really any question?

Personal Development Goals:

Business/Career goals:

Toys/Adventure Goals:

Contribution Goals:

5

---◆---

ESTABLISHING EMOTIONAL SELF-CONTROL

Within the first couple of months, I noticed that I was beginning to take control of myself. Although I was not making much financial progress little things no longer bugged me the way they used to. When someone cut in front of me in traffic, I used Tony's techniques to stay calm. When my car got towed away, I managed to find reasons this might be a good thing. When my basketball team lost in the playoffs to Michael Jordan, I did not stay in a bad mood for long. My thinking was starting to help me stay in a positive frame of mind.

Unfortunately, there were no teachers in high school or college who taught me how to master my psychology. Yes, they taught me how to multiply numbers and the capital of Ecuador, but they did not teach the most important thing I have learned so far:

How to think properly and
manage my emotional states.

Obviously, some people have been able to learn these things through trial and error and have succeeded brilliantly without ever consulting any type of personal development program. But I certainly did not and I would guess that most people have not. In *Personal Power*, Tony gives us many techniques for mastering our psychology. This is what his course is primarily about: the science of success conditioning.

The Power of "Right" Thinking

Although *Personal Power* can certainly lead to a lot of money, I believe that Tony's main purpose is to get you to start thinking the "right way," so you can accomplish anything that your mind sets as a goal. One of my favorite lines from *Back to the Future* is when Marty (Michael J. Fox) tells his dad when he is still in high school, "If you put your mind to it, you can accomplish anything." By the end of the movie, you see how this one new belief changed his life in the revised future thirty years later. Rather than becoming the geeky subordinate to the neighborhood bully, he instead becomes the author of a science fiction novel, simply through adding that one quality belief to his thinking. You don't need a time machine to change your future. By changing your beliefs today, just imagine what you will be able to accomplish, ten, twenty and thirty years from now.

I sometimes try to imagine where I would be today had I started Tony's program when I was twelve or thirteen. I probably would have been as cool as Ferris Bueller in high school. ˙(Remember, he knew exactly what he was going to do when he woke up that morning.) Perhaps I could have gone to Harvard or

Yale because I would have been more focused on being the best I could be. But I'll leave that for my kids who will be listening to Tony Robbins when they are still in diapers. For now, I am just thankful that I started when I did and that I've been able to design a life that I'm excited to be living every day.

Let's discuss the principles I used to help master my psychology. (Of course I still have my bad days – but I'm now able to keep them to a minimum.)

Opting for Self-Control

The first step I took was deciding to take control of the relationship with myself. After reading the book and listening to the tapes you get the feeling that you can actually be in control of your thinking. This will give you the confidence to tell yourself what you need to do to become successful. The more positive days you have, the greater your success momentum will be. Instead of having three good days and four bad days, you will have five great days and two mediocre days. It does not take much to get ahead. If you manage to spend more than half of your time being outstanding, then you will be able to create a happier and more productive life.

Let's look for a moment at relationships, in general. An excellent relationship is one where you are happy 80 – 90 percent of the time. It makes the other 10 – 20 percent something that you can recover from since you are happy with your significant other most of the time. However, if you are happy only 10 – 20 percent of the time, the other 80 – 90 percent will eventually kill the relationship. Why would you want to spend time and effort on something that is good only 10 percent of the time? It's the same with the relationship you have with yourself. If you are able to manage your mental state and are happy/productive more often than not, then you will be way ahead of someone who lacks that kind of self-control. Success breeds success. When you achieve small accomplishments you will gain the confidence to strive for bigger ones.

Asking Yourself Better Questions

I was able to take control of myself by implementing several of Tony's strategies. One is ask myself better questions. This worked especially well to put me in the right frame of mind. As you read the excerpts I include from my journal, you'll see that I often use questions to resolve any situation. The first example is from when I first started and the second is from seven years later. Both will give you an idea of what you can do when you need a mental boost. (In the beginning, it's best to do this almost every day – if not on paper, at least in your head on your way to work.)

1992
What is great in life right now?
1) *I have just completed a success program* (Personal Power) *that will help me reach my goals.*
2) *I have a higher paying job than I did six months ago.*
3) *I have a pretty decent place to live which I can fix up to be better.*
4) *I am in a good relationship with someone who has supported me when I was unemployed.*

5) *I have three great dogs that are very happy to see me every day.*

6) *I have re-established my relationship with my parents, although it still needs much improvement.*

7) *I believe that I am a great salesman who has a lot of potential to Make it Big!*

8) *I know that I have the intellectual capability to handle most situations, as I scored in the top 5 percent on the GMAT.*

9) *I have a car that is in great working condition that I managed to get for very little money down.*

10) *I feel like I am on my way up after hitting rock bottom. There is nowhere to go but UP!*

Remember that I wrote this just a few months after being at rock bottom. It shows that I was relatively upbeat for the situation. The best part is that I had hope and something to be happy about each day, no matter how my reality may have compared to my goals at the time. If you have not done so already, I recommend that you stop reading and immediately take Tony's advice to write down ten things that are great (or could be great) in your life right now.

◆ What is great in my life right now? ◆

1)

2)

3)

4)

5)

6)

7)

8)

9)

10)

How do you feel? If you took this exercise seriously, I suspect you feel a lot better than before you started. Please don't write this down on just any scrap of paper. If you don't want to write in this book (I know – I was taught the same thing back in grade school), do it in a success journal. If you don't have one, get one. Who knows? You may someday be copying from it for a book called "Thank You, Tony Robbins, Too."

The Pleasure of Seeing Your Progress

Trust me, you will love reading things you wrote five years ago – because you will see how much you've grown. You will be amazed how often you go back to reading your earlier journals because it is so exciting to see your progress.

Here is what I wrote in 1999:

What is great in my life right now?

1) *I am control of my destiny – I do what I want and when I want – Nobody tells me what to do except me.*

2) *I have my own law offices in Los Angeles and Las Vegas which are making enough money so I can do what I want.*

3) *I have a great relationship with a girl that I am very excited about. We love each other a lot!*

4) *I have gone to Maui three times in the past nine months and got to see the whales.*

5) *I just came back from Europe where we had an amazing time. Got to go to some great restaurants and drink a bottle of wine during every dinner (something I could not afford when I went there in 1995).*

6) *I have been running since 1995 and am in the best shape of my life.*

7) *I have improved my relationship with my parents. I was able to write an article that was published to thank them for all their love and support – most importantly, to let them know how I feel.*

8) *I have improved my lawyering skills and feel confident going to court. Just finished my first appeal, which I won. My client thought I was the best thing since sliced bread.*

9) *I am driving a BMW that I am very excited about. It was once only a goal written in my success journal. I didn't think I could ever buy a nice car again because my credit was terrible for a couple of years.*

10) *I am still trying to improve in all areas so that I can make constant and never-ending improvement. Remember, if you are not climbing, you are sliding.*

I still get excited when I review my past journals. At the very least, it reminds me that I have the ability to make real accomplishments and energizes me for my current goals. As you can see, there is great power in asking yourself, "What is great in my life right now?"

As I said before, these exercises offer you a great place to solve problems. Prior to my Robbins experience, I used to respond to problems and challenges with negative open-ended questions such as, "Why does this keep happening to me?" or "Why am I such a loser?" Naturally, questions like these can only increase your negativity.

Negative Questions and Positive Questions

Back in college, I remember being interested in a particular girl. When she left me a message on Wednesday canceling our Friday date, I immediately started asking myself why she didn't want to go out with me. I came up with such reasons as:

1) She must not think I am very attractive.
2) She must have found out something bad about me.
3) She must have gone back to her old boyfriend.
4) She must have met someone new at the mixer she went to last night.
5) She must have got a better offer for Friday night.
6) I must have said something stupid during our last conversation.
7) She must have seen me talking to another girl in one of my classes and thinks I am cheating on her.

Haven't we all done something stupid like this? To make things worse, I kept repeating these answers to myself during the next 24 hours till the next time I got to speak to her. Not only did my negative self-talk put me in a bad mood, I was extremely unproductive that whole next day. I paid no attention in my classes, did no homework and had no fun at all. I'm sure something like this has happened to all of us. I kept asking myself that same negative question over and over again. Naturally, it never elicited a positive response, since it presupposed a negative answer.

I'm sure you can guess what happened next. When I finally got a chance to speak to my friend, she said that she needed to move our date to Saturday. It turned out that her parents were visiting and she wanted to spend some quality time with them. Which left me to contemplate all that wasted time and unnecessary misery.

I should have asked myself a different question, e.g., What might have come up for her to postpone our date? Look at the choice of words: "postpone." It implies that our date was going to take place – just at a different time. Also, why not presuppose that nothing is wrong with you and that something in her agenda must have necessitated the change. Had I used what Tony teaches, I would not have wasted an entire day worrying about it.

Focusing on Solutions

It is natural for us to focus on the negative when things start to go wrong. This is probably part of our survival instinct. Back in the caveman days, when a problem surfaced you needed to beware of all the bad things that could happen, in order to avoid getting eaten by dinosaurs. In the 21st century we don't need to do that. What we do need is to ask ourselves a better quality of question when a challenge comes up. Tony suggests the following:

1) What can I do right now to resolve this problem?
2) What could be great about this problem?
3) What great things could happen as a result of my new situation?

You will be surprised how well this process works for resolving problems. When you ask questions like this your mind starts working on the solution instead of focusing on the problem. It also allows you to take charge of the situation.

Let's look at a typical problem that many of us have faced. Perhaps you have been fired or laid off from a job in your past. How did you handle it? Did you ask yourself the right questions? As I discussed earlier, I've had a great many jobs in my lifetime. In fact, I had sixteen different ones during my first four years out of college. And you thought *you* couldn't stay with a job for a long time!

My jobs were: working for a car rental company, working for a consumer loan company, selling advertising binders, selling consumer products from business to business, working as an adjuster for an insurance company, leasing apartments, working as a property accountant for five different real estate management companies, and working as a salesman for five different real estate sales offices. Whatever your job history, it is unlikely to be worse than mine.

During my checkered employment history, I did not ask the

right questions and often got down on myself. After being fired or quitting, I would often ask myself questions like:

1) Why am I such a big loser?
2) How come I never can keep a job?
3) Why can't I ever succeed?
4) Why didn't I go to graduate school?
5) Why didn't my parents help me out more?

How could anyone possibly improve his situation by asking these questions? Fortunately, I completed Tony's tape program before I was "let go" by a company that sold long distance services. Rather than getting down on myself, I started asking quality questions:

1) What could be great about this?
2) How can I use this to get closer to my goals?
3) What can I do to make myself feel good right now?
4) What could I have done to improve myself so this would not have happened?
5) What can I do in the future to ensure that I will have the type of job I can enjoy and work hard on?

The answers I got helped me arrive where I am ten years later. I could easily have wallowed in self-pity and made things worse. However, I used this as an opportunity to apply what I had learned from Tony Robbins. This was the first real setback I had faced since discovering his program and I was anxious to see if his stuff really worked. Thank God it did. Here are the answers I gave to the above questions:

1) The great part is that I really hated my job and was only staying because I desperately needed the money.

2) *Another great thing is that I have the opportunity to look for a higher paying job, one that I can enjoy more than the previous job.*

3) *This will give me the time to think more seriously about designing a life I can be excited about.*

4) *I can spend my extra time learning more about success, reviewing Tony's tape program and reading* Awaken the Giant Within.

5) *I can use this to get closer to my goals by seeing this job as a stepping-stone to greater things in my future. I know that someday I will be in business for myself. I will try to learn as much as possible about how to establish my own business in the upcoming months.*

6) *I can make myself feel good right now by: listening to my Tony Robbins tapes, writing in my success journal, listening to my favorite music or going to see a funny movie.*

This enabled me to focus on a solution while at the same time maintaining an uplifting mood. It would have been difficult to come up with solutions if I were not in the right frame of mind. That needs to come first. If you have the right attitude, you will be in a better position to take positive action. With these answers I was able to make it through this crisis and secure another job. My next job was nothing to get excited about, but at least it paid me an additional $750 per month. Also, I did not have to drive 45 miles each way just to get to the office. It allowed me to work from home several days per week. Nothing earth shattering, but a clear improvement.

Initially, don't expect mega changes overnight. Success

usually takes some time. Although I knew this next job wasn't my ultimate dream, I now had more confidence about handling problems and coming up with solutions. Asking the right type of question breeds great thinking. As human beings we have an ability that no other species on this earth has: the ability to think about more than mere survival. However, most people get caught up in their daily routines and never really tap into this potential. Think about it: what new ideas did you come up with today that could move you closer to your dream life?

Some of you may do this every day without consciously using these Tony Robbins questions. More power to you. But I'm willing to bet that most of us need some guidance to develop this skill. I consider myself a fairly well educated person, but I did not employ these strategies before *Personal Power*.

The questions I asked once I was in that new position greatly helped me design and obtain the life I always wanted. Rather than continually asking, "Why do I have do such a crappy job?" I asked, "What can I learn from this job that will help me be in business for myself?" As it turned out, I did learn to be a great salesperson. By diligently practicing the sales techniques and communication skills they taught, I was able to develop the rainmaking abilities I needed to establish my own business. I also learned about maintaining the proper cash reserves and budget forecasting that are essential to any start-up endeavor. By asking the right questions and knowing my ultimate outcome (my own business), I was able to focus on the things that could help me reach my big dream.

As Tony says, when you know what you want and why you want it, you activate your nervous system to notice the right things. I am sure that if you have ever decided to buy a particular car, you see many more of them on the street. This is not because people suddenly started buying more of them, but because you have activated your nervous system to be on the alert for what you want. The key is to activate your nervous system to your big dream. Only then will you truly be on your way. The first step you have to make before you can accomplish anything really big is to take control of yourself.

6

◆

USING YOUR PHYSIOLOGY TO GET IN A PEAK STATE

Using my body to control my emotions and energy was not something I was ever taught. My energy and excitement were always the result of what was happening around me. If things were going well, I would be energized. For instance, if I made a sale and a big commission, I would crank up my stereo and jump up and down. Or, when the Los Angeles Lakers or the Dodgers would win a big game I would be screaming at the top of my lungs, cheering them on.

It's easy to feel good when things are going well around you. You don't need any effort to behave differently. It just happens naturally. The real trick is how to achieve this state when things aren't going well. An important lesson Tony teaches is that we can create these moments on a regular basis, regardless of what is happening in the world. Even when our favorite team loses or we have just failed to close a big sale, Tony teaches us how to reach that good feeling. His message is that emotion is created by motion. All the good or bad states we feel result from how we use our bodies.

Do you recall the last time you were feeling a little low? I'll bet you had a frown on your face and your head was down. More than likely, your voice lacked energy. Contrast this to when you were feeling on top of the world. Quite a difference, huh? I'll also bet you were never taught that you could change the way you felt simply by incorporating a few "power moves," as Tony calls them. Or simply by cranking up your stereo and jumping up and down for no reason. Most of us are taught that we shouldn't do those things unless we have some occasion to do so. Tony teaches the opposite: we should consciously try to move our bodies in ways that make us feel good even when we have absolutely no reason to. In fact, we should be doing this *especially* when we are feeling down.

How "Power Moves" Work

When I began to employ Tony's techniques, this was all new to me.   Since I was at rock bottom, I desperately needed something to believe in. *Personal Power* teaches you to experiment with both positive and negative body movements and postures. You are instructed to sit up straight and alert with a big smile on your face. Tony then asks his listeners to see if they can get depressed with a big smile on their faces. The answer is no! It is difficult to "feel" depressed when your physical body is acting otherwise. Conversely, we are instructed to put a frown on our face, take shallow breaths and slouch. It is hard to feel good with your body in those positions.

The next step is to design a power move to get you pumped up and in a peak state on demand. (Tony basically gets us to turn ourselves "on" whenever we want.) For me, the movement was pumping my fist, saying *"yes," "I'm the man," "I rock."* (By the way, I started doing this fist pump long before Tiger made it fashionable.) It worked. Despite what was happening in my life, I could literally put myself in a good mood by following a ritual that consisted of: cranking up loud music, jumping up and down, smiling incessantly (like Tom Cruise) or doing my "Tiger" fist pump.

I started using this in a variety of situations. The first was when I really wanted to get out of a down mood. If I was feeling blue, I simply did some of my power moves. Say my basketball team just lost a big playoff game. My normal reaction would be to feel a little deflated for a couple of hours after the game. Usually this state wouldn't wear off until I got back into my normal routine. This is where Tony's method comes in. After a big loss like that, I consciously made a decision to change my state. I would turn off the T.V. and crank up the music. I would dance like a crazed fool. Or, I would use my fist pumping. Anything to get my body moving in a positive direction. To make it even more powerful, I combined it with Tony's power questions to change my focus. And whammo! (Tony's word!)

My defeated mood was instantly changed into a fun and energized state that focused on all the good things going on in my life. You don't even need to get this crazy. I observed my father-in-law unconsciously employing some of Tony's techniques during our last visit. The Buffalo Bills were playing a great game until the fourth quarter when they blew a big lead. It was a devastating loss, especially for this die-hard fan. I recall him getting up out of his chair and excusing himself to go out for a short walk. When he returned, his mind was clear and he was back to his jovial self. Rather than wallow around in the loss, he changed his state instantly by taking a strategic walk and focusing on other things. I doubt he did this as a result of listening to a Tony Robbins CD, but the principle was certainly the same.

The best part is that you don't need to keep doing these moves for hours. Shifting your mood requires only a few minutes. Another familiar situation I faced was getting pumped up for something extremely important. Let's say I had a sales appointment with a company president, and this one sale would make my month. Previously, I might have gone into that meeting a little intimidated, with my body reflecting much of my doubt and tension. It's hard to perform at your best when your body and mind are not in a peak state.

As Tony described in *Personal Power*, you don't want to hit against Dwight Gooden (when he was great) if you're not in a peak state. Similarly, you don't want to go into an important sales presentation when you're not at your best. Tony's technique really helped me in that situation. Before going into that type of meeting, I would sit in my car for a few extra minutes, cranking up my favorite song, pumping my fist and saying good things about myself. Yes, I might have looked a little strange to passers-by, but I would go into the meeting feeling great. I might not have made the sale every time, but I certainly put myself in a much better position to close the deal. Also, this technique made it much easier to recover from a failed attempt. I can't tell you how much this strategy has helped me during the past ten years.

I remember taking a rest room break during the bar exam. We were about four hours into a six-hour exam. Naturally, I was feeling a little spent. But I went into that bathroom, looked into the mirror and pumped my fist. I said out loud, "You're the man, you will kick ass, you can beat these people! You studied hard, go back in there and dominate!" Okay I might have looked a little stupid. I might even have felt a little ridiculous. But you know what? I'd rather look a little foolish and pass the exam. The choice is yours. You have to be a little outrageous to be better than everyone else. Tony is the most outrageous motivational speaker I have ever heard. Do you think he is worried about how he looks? (Not when he looks at his bank account!)

Use this method of getting pumped up prior to all of your "big moments." The next time you are about to call the girl or guy of your dreams, take a few minutes to get into a peak state. Or just before a big interview. Why would you ever want to do something important in less than your peak state? I've heard that even Tony still goes through a ritual before he goes on stage for a seminar. He does a series of incantations in which he tells himself that he is going to make a difference and touch people's lives.

Don't be surprised if the power of movement makes a dramatic change in your life. Start with something small if you are skeptical. Tony recommends that we smile for one full minute, five times per day. Try it! It isn't going to cost you anything. Instead of lighting up a cigarette or having a drink to change your state, why don't you try a smile. If you've ever watched *Ally McBeal,* you know that one of the two founding partners, John Cage (The Biscuit), employs smile therapy whenever a conflict arises. A simple thing like this can make an enormous difference in your life.

Laughter as a Power Move

If you want to take the smile thing a step further, you can include some laughter. Studies have shown that laughter actually stimulates our immune system. Think about it. Have you ever met a depressed person who laughed often? It's really hard to stay depressed when you are laughing a lot. Did you ever notice how a funny movie lifted you right out of your depression? In reality, nothing in your life changed while you were sitting in that theater. We all need to laugh more often.

When I was at rock bottom I really didn't want to see anything funny, wasn't "in the mood" for a comedy. It was only after I became aware of the power of laughter that I deliberately went to see a comedy when I wasn't in the mood. Even the type of music you listen to can contribute to depression. I don't know if you are familiar with The Smiths or Morrissey (kind of depressing music), but I listened to those artists quite a bit during my down times. I never really listened to dance music or anything with an "up" tempo at these times. I figured that since I was depressed, I should do everything in my power to keep my environment the same way. Boy, would Tony have slapped me around! I was doing exactly the opposite of what I needed to do to get out of the funk I was in.

Even after listening to *Personal Power*, it took several years before many of my goals started to become a reality. Fortunately, I learned early on to keep myself in a great mood and a peak state, even though my surroundings had not yet changed for the better. Since money was tight, I wasn't able to go to a lot of movies (especially at night). However, I was fortunate to have a ninety-nine-cent video store close by, and I rented three or four comedies every week to keep me a good mood. The results were fabulous. Instead of coming home from a frustrating day of work to even more stress, I changed my state with some comedy. Now I'm not advocating that you spend all day in front of the TV set. However, if you can't afford to go out and do many fun things, it is highly therapeutic to spend 90 minutes on a hilarious movie. This may not sound too glamorous, but it worked for me. Depression became a rarity for me and my positive momentum grew even more. You need to find whatever elevates your spirits and keeps you in a peak state.

Even now, when things are going well for me most of the time, I still employ Tony's laughter techniques. Whenever I feel down, I move quickly to limit the damage. I still like to go to a funny movie. I recall the last time I lost a big trial. (Yes, I have experienced defeat – and so has Tony – so don't feel alone!) I remember walking to the parking lot feeling defeated. My slumped shoulders and discouraged expression told the story. I moped around for about an hour until I realized this wasn't very Tony Robbins-esque of me. I told myself that I had made it through bigger disappointments in the past. Furthermore, I now knew how to make myself feel good employing Tony's techniques.

Although I was initially fighting it, I tried to smile. I turned the CD player on full blast to my favorite Will Smith song, *Getting Jiggy With It!,* and danced in my car seat. People driving by must have thought I was nuts. I got home and told my fiancée we were going out. We went to see an extremely funny movie, *Meet the Parents*, I laughed so hard that tears came to my eyes. Presto! By the time the movie ended, I had forgotten that I lost the trial. I had a big smile on my face, giggling as we talked about some of the lines from the movie. Tony's techniques really work.

Think of what I could have done had I not made a conscious effort to change my state. I might have gone home focusing on my defeat, could have maintained that morose expression on my face all night. I could have been a terrible person to be with. Worst of all, I could have had a miserable time for the next several days. But I decided to take control of my destiny and how I felt. My evening (or life) was not dependent on what those twelve jurors said about my client. (In retrospect, I believe they did do the right thing.) Only I should decide how I'm going to feel and act. Instead of being a jerk that night, my fiancée (now wife) commented on how much fun I was especially for someone who had just lost a two-week trial. Isn't it amazing what we can do with ourselves?

◆ Assignment ◆

The next time you have a miserable day, make a conscious effort to have a super-fun, entertaining evening. Surprise everyone by how happy you are, despite your trying circumstances. You will really impress those around you and you might even impress *yourself.*

7

---◆---

MAKING THE
RIGHT DECISIONS

In Tony's book *Awaken the Giant Within* he discusses the importance of decisions. He writes: "It is in your moments of decision that your destiny is shaped." Think about it. Your decision to pig out at dinner, night after night, has made you forty pounds overweight. Your decision to do drugs has caused you to waste all your money and get fired from your job. Your decision to watch television all evening, instead of attending night school, has caused you to remain in that job you hate. Your decision not to exercise has caused you to get tired after climbing a flight of stairs (and greatly increased your chances of getting a heart attack). Your decision to drop out of high school has caused you to have limited job opportunities. Your decision to spend all your time at the office and neglect your spouse has caused her to cheat on you.

I know some of you may be saying that someone else caused you to be where you are today. An abusive parent, a husband who beat you, or an unexpected child may be your excuse for your current predicament. But the truth is, what you decided to do with your situation has put you where you are. There are many men and women who have succeeded despite having a child in their teens. There are many women who have escaped abusive husbands. And there are many people who have succeeded despite having parents that were both physically and sexually abusive.

The best example of this is one that Tony often mentions: Oprah Winfrey. Oprah had a lot of strikes against her. She was abused as a child. She got pregnant when she was a teenager. Add to that she was a black woman at a time in history when both her race and her gender limited her opportunities. Not only did she manage to survive, she is now one of America's great success stories. Always in the top five on the highest paid entertainer list, she makes hundreds of millions of dollars every year. Her television show is one that communicates the idea that each and every one of us has a potential for success.

She made the right decision. She decided that she would succeed even though her odds for success were not great. It would have been easy for her to say, "It's no use, I've got all these strikes against me, I should just give up and accept what life has given me."

Tony Robbins also made a major decision. When he was at rock bottom, listening to Neil Diamond in his 400-square-foot bachelor apartment, he decided to stop settling for where he was in life. He could have been one of the many unknown Joes out there who just kept eating his potato chips, sitting on the couch watching "General Hospital." Luckily for us, he chose to set a higher standard. Although I have learned about personal achievement from other great writers and speakers, it was Tony's

Personal Power program that helped me make the *decision to commit to a program of success.*

Making the Big Decision

After you make that decision, it changes your destiny. Even small decisions, once set in motion, can result in incredible benefits decades later. Remember in *Back to the Future,* when George McFly (thanks to the advice and counseling of his son, Marty – a kid with Tony Robbins qualities) decides to stand up to the bully, Biff, and knocks him out with one punch. This one act changed his future: from being Biff's employee to becoming Biff's boss. In life, as well as in fiction, a small decision can set off a whole chain of events, an alternate future.

Think of where you would be today had you made a few different decisions. If you had joined that gym and worked out twice a week, you would now have that great body you are dreaming of. If you had gone to business school at night instead of vegging out in front of your TV, you could be the manager of your department. If you had spent enough quality time with your spouse, you might still have the great relationship you once had. If you had spent quality time with your children, they would still be speaking to you. Decisions like these have enormous consequences later.

The good news is: it's never too late to make the *right* decisions. Although I often regret not having made better decisions earlier in my life, I am comforted by the results of having made the right decision ten years ago to follow Tony's program for success. Whether you are fifteen or fifty, the sooner you start making the right decisions, the sooner you will have a life you have designed that you can be excited about and proud of.

Let's look at some positive decisions that have shaped our world as we know it today. What if Bill Gates had decided not to drop out of Harvard in order to develop DOS? Would I have been writing this book on a typewriter instead of a laptop computer? What if John F. Kennedy had decided to follow the advice of some of his "war monger" cohorts during the Cuban missle crisis? Would there be parts of our country contaminated with radioactive debris? What if Thomas Edison had given up on the electric light bulb? Would I be writing this by candlelight? What if our founding fathers decided they could not defeat England and gain our independence? Would we be bowing to a king instead counting votes (and then recounting) for a President?

Starting From Where You Are

Begin with something small and work your way up. Decide not to finish everything on your plate. Decide to take a fifteen-minute walk. Decide to talk to your kids about their homework. Decide to tell your spouse, "I love you," more than once a year. That doesn't sound too difficult, does it?

After you begin feeling confident about making small decisions, try some bigger ones. Decide to work out five times per week. Decide to enroll in night school so you can get the degree that will increase your opportunities for advancement. Decide to go to Paris because you have been dreaming about it your entire life. Decide to start saving extra money every month so you can stop renting and buy a home. Remember, it all starts with a decision. And the best part is, you have total control over your decision making. Even if you have a terrible boss at work, no one can stop you from improving your skills and knowledge by attending night school. Even if you are fifty pounds overweight, no one can tell you that you cannot start working out every day. Even if you are stuck in a job you hate, no one can prevent you from exploring ways to start your own business in the future. It is invigorating to realize that you alone can shape your destiny simply by making better decisions.

Three Destiny-Shaping Questions

Tony takes decision making to another level when he says that three decisions control your ultimate destiny:

1) Your decision about what to focus on
2) Your decision about what things mean
3) Your decision about what to do to create the results that you want

Deciding What to Focus On

During the past ten years these guidelines have not only helped me achieve many of the goals I set out to accomplish, they have also kept me in a quality frame of mind. I especially like the way Tony describes the importance of your decision about what to focus on. He talks about someone filming various happenings at a typical party. In different parts of the house you can have people who are arguing, people making out and really connecting, people dancing and jumping around because of the great music, and someone crying because a jerk just broke up with her. Depending on what you want to focus on at the party, you can get feelings of happiness, sadness, excitement, passion or anger. The same is true for your life. At any given moment you can focus on all the good things that are happening to you or on all the bad things.

Applying this concept to my own mental states, I started focusing on the positive part of the party (my life) and began to experience a greater sense of happiness. For instance, I decided to focus on:

1) I was alive and in good health.
2) I graduated from high school and college with pretty good grades.
3) I was in a relationship with someone who loved me.
4) I had a place to live and a working automobile
5) I had a job.
6) I had a few really good friends – who stuck with me despite my screw-ups.
7) My family still cared a lot about me.
8) I knew that I had the potential to do much better.
9) I managed to get hold of *Personal Power* even though I didn't have a credit card.
10) I believed that I had already hit rock bottom and was on my way up.

The point of this is not to make you so content that you will give up on your dreams. On the contrary, before you can get to the next level, you have to be happy where you are. When you are in a positive state you will be better able to handle the challenges that will arise on the way to your goals. This is not merely positive thinking, but a way to get the most from your current situation. Do you think that you will be better motivated to do some extra studying/running/working when you are in a good mood or when you are in a bad mood? Well, put yourself in a great mood by focusing on the all the positive things happening in your life right now. As Tony says, it is better to "happily achieve, than achieve to be happy." Why would you want to wait till you accomplish a major goal before you allow yourself to be happy? Be happy now, and it will be a whole lot easier to reach your goals.

Deciding What Things Mean

Instead of being depressed about the things I did not have, I chose to make a different decision about what things in my life really meant.

1) The fact that I had a job that enabled me to pay my bills (instead of how terrible the job was).

2) How lucky I was to watch a great basketball game (instead of the fact that my team lost).

3) Having food on the table (instead of the fact that I rarely went out for dinner).

4) The many sunny days in Los Angeles (instead of the fact that it is raining today).

5) All the great things about my current relationship (instead of all the hot girls out there that I was missing out on).

Deciding What To Do To Create the Results You Want

The answers I obtained from the first two questions put me in a powerful state. A motivated state. From there, the last step was deciding what to do to create the results I wanted in my life. Since I knew what I wanted from the detailed goal-setting workshop I discussed in Chapter Four, I had to brainstorm and determine what needed to be done to reach those goals. As you have read, one of my major goals was to control my own destiny. I continually asked myself, "What do I need to do to control my own destiny?" This question did not have a simple of list of answers like the previous two. Rather, it led to a web of questions and answers that evolved over a period of time. This is what went on in my thoughts:

In order to be master of my own destiny I need to call the shots. I need to have my own business, where I'm the boss. How can I have my own business? I need either some skill or trade that I can sell to others or some capital to start a business of my own. I don't know where I could get that capital. My credit is really bad right now. Could I borrow any money from friends or relatives? Unlikely.

Do I have any skills that I could market right now? I have sales skills, but I would need to work for someone else because I don't have the capital to sell my own products. Could I go out and learn a marketable skill? Yes, but I would have to go back to school. Do I want to go back to school? Not really. Are there any other ways I could start my own business? I did see that guy on TV talk about making money in real estate with no money down. But someone told me that doesn't work so well in Los Angeles.

What about this school option? My parents did say they would help me out if I wanted to go to law school. But I don't think I can study for the LSAT. I gave up last time and felt like a big loser. Is there any other way I can control my own destiny? Not really. Am I sure that I need to control my own destiny? Absolutely. Can I be happy the way I am right now? Not totally. I want to have a life where I can do what I want when I want.

Don't give up so fast. If you really need to study hard I'm sure you can. It's worth another shot, isn't it? So what if you have to study hard. Would you rather keep working for this vending machine company? No! The idea of being lawyer with my own practice sounds exciting. I know several lawyers who are doing quite well. Tony says I need to make the right decision about what to do to create the results I want. I want to control my own destiny. Let's go for it!

These paragraphs summarizing my thoughts about my future probably took you only a minute or two to read, but the process of making this crucial decision actually took me over a year. It was certainly not an easy task. Nothing worthwhile ever is. The key is to continually ask yourself: "What do I need to do to create the results I want?" And then make the decision to do it.

8

◆

THE
STRUGGLE UPWARD

Some of you reading this book may think that my transformation from less than zero to someone in control of his own destiny came easily. Let me squash that belief right now. It might look on paper like a smooth transition, but it required a lot of struggle, especially in the beginning. Even after completing *Personal Power* and reading *Awaken the Giant Within,* I still faced incredibly trying times. Remember, I am writing this book after a decade of following Tony's strategies. I'm not telling this to discourage you, but rather to remind you that your journey can be filled with many pitfalls and still arrive at the goals you deeply desire.

As I mentioned earlier, the first big challenge I faced after completing Tony's program was that I was laid off (to put it gently) by a company selling long distance services. I confess that this was quite a blow, because I desperately needed the $1,000 per month I was being paid, just to make ends meet. In retrospect, I must admit that I deserved to be terminated by that company. Although I was meeting my quota and was even top salesman for several months, I had a bad attitude that did not serve the company's best interest. I believed I was too good to have to follow their procedures. Now that might have been so, but they were in charge, not me. If I expected them to pay me, I should have respected their rules.

I was so desperate for a paycheck that I went to see the company president within a couple of days and begged for my job back. I recall that day vividly. A friend and his wife were visiting from out of town. We had some plans that included going to Disneyland and the San Diego Zoo. I had been fired two days before they arrived. Too embarrassed to say I was terminated, I pretended to have the week off. On our way to San Diego, I dropped them off at a restaurant for lunch and told them I was going to stop into work for a few minutes. That is when I tried to get my job back. Fortunately I now see, my boss refused to re-hire me. Remembering myself actually begging for a job that I hated, I realize that my self-respect was at an all-time low.

The next couple of months were extremely difficult. Even with my new-found knowledge from Tony Robbins, I still experienced periods of despair. Even though I hated my job, it had still provided me with the esteem of earning a paycheck. Immersing myself with Tony's tapes and books, I began to use my success journal on a daily basis, writing down as many positive tidbits as possible.

After several weeks of wallowing in self-pity, I resolved to get another job. Money was running out and I needed to find something fast. But nothing seemed to pan out. I went on over forty interviews for various sales jobs and got rejected each time. The companies willing to take me on offered only jobs that paid straight commission. With my tight financial situation, I couldn't afford to wait a few more months with no money coming in. I had an interview every other day and the days seemed to drag on. It was easy to go from motivated to depressed. Although I saw no immediate results, my success journal at least kept me from going over the edge. It provided me with some kind of hope when everything was coming back negative on the job front.

These were not dream jobs I was applying for. I was looking for *any* job that put some money in my pocket. I interviewed for jobs such as: selling pagers, leasing office equipment such as copiers and postage meters, selling auto parts to various dealerships, selling vacuum cleaners, selling advertising space, and selling Chevrolet cars. (I initially got the last one but was later rejected for having poor credit!) This was all highly discouraging. Hadn't I gone to college for four years? What was I doing, seven years out of college with no job or marketable skills? What had happened?

My lack of a job not only affected my pocketbook, it started to hurt my relationships with those close to me. Many of my friends of similar age had begun to achieve wealth, recognition and managerial status through their career pursuits. I started avoiding these people. Not because I didn't like them. But hearing their accomplishments only reminded me of how little I had done. There came a point where the pleasure of their company was exceeded by the ever-present reminder of my own perceived failure.

So there I was, with no job and diminished personal relationships. Obviously there was virtually no money available for fun. I recall telling some friends who invited me to a movie that I really couldn't afford to go at night. Even matinees were a stretch. Entertainment was having two dollars in quarters and walking over to my local 7-11 to play the *Adams Family* or *Terminator II* pinball machines. Now remember, I was seven years out of college and without any kids to feed. Yes, it was a lifestyle that refugees in Afghanistan could only dream about, but they didn't have all the opportunities I'd had. The knowledge of that wasted potential was the most painful part.

It was during those days that I made a firm commitment to follow Tony's program. Although I had diligently reviewed his material earlier, I was not 100 percent committed. Perhaps I needed to be at rock bottom with no hope in sight, to fully hear Tony's voice. When I was doing relatively okay, I thought these "success" oriented programs were for the weak. Once I was seriously committed to follow Tony's success program, my journal started becoming more interactive. Instead of merely serving as a notebook to take down what I had learned from the books and tapes, it became a place where I could write down my goals and strategies for achieving them. As I described in Chapter Five, it became a place to ask and answer some tough questions. This didn't happen overnight, but gradually over the span of several weeks. Here's a sample of what I wrote:

Why will I succeed? (And why failure is good?)

1)   *I am now committed to work harder than someone who hasn't tasted failure.*
2)   *No choice but to succeed. I can't be happy without success.*
3)   *Failure has pissed me off so much.*
4)   *I have proven to myself that I can succeed in the past.*

5) *I am more determined than someone who hasn't experienced major setbacks.*

6) *I know how to handle failure in the future.*

What do I need to do?

1) *Work harder than anyone else to make up for my past screwups.*

2) *Focus on making $100,000/year every day!*

3) *Don't be scared of past debts and problems. If you make money these problems will be solved.*

4) *Need to get cocky confidence.*

5) *Need to get an attitude that my life is great!*

6) *Work Hard/Play Hard.*

Although I had all these thoughts in mind, I really needed to get them on paper so I could review them on a daily basis. This way, today's inspiration doesn't become tomorrow's dim memory. This thinking was something totally different than I was used to and it needed to become a new way of life. You can't just wish your way to having a quality life. You must take active steps toward achieving it. That is what Tony instilled in me.

After several months of consistent rejection I finally got a new job. It wasn't anything great (leasing vending machines), but it served a valuable purpose in my overall development. The next step was to be able to succeed at this new job. It certainly wasn't easy. Although I got paid a weekly salary, I could have been fired within months if I hadn't produced. I saw other "trainees" being canned after only three months when they couldn't cut it. In the past, I would have done the minimum to get by. However, this was a new beginning. Here's an excerpt from my journal:

> *Completed the initial three day training program and did extremely well. I scored 100% on all tests and got an "A" for my final grade while everyone else got B's and C's. I feel excited about the program I am going to represent, but more importantly, I am excited about my enthusiasm and hard work I am putting in. My new belief is that success will come as the result of hard work. I believe this is the first training class (and I have been in many!) that I put forth a 100% effort in everything – which says a lot about the past twenty-eight years.*
>
> *I really think I needed to experience the pain and failure of my previous beliefs in order to change to the proper ones. I feel that my new belief system will lead me to greater successes than could have been possible had I not experienced the failures of the past two years. I now believe the past two years of failure were necessary to mold me into the successful giant I know I will become in the future.*

As we all know, success in the classroom doesn't always make for sales in the real world. Despite my efforts to learn how to give an effective presentation, I had not made a sale in the first two months. Worse yet, the other three guys in my class – who got lower grades – were all able to make sales. I was getting quite frustrated and a little uneasy about my job status. If I hadn't been so motivated and so obviously committed (quite a contrast from my previous job), I think they would have fired me before I made my first sale. This is where Tony's lessons on massive failure helped a lot. After each failed attempt I kept telling myself that "massive failure equals success." I needed to keep reminding myself of why I was going to succeed. I think the fact that the other guys in my class made sales before me was a great good for me. I kept thinking that if they could do it, so could I. I mean, I clearly knew my stuff better than they did. My manager even told me that several times. My sales skills were actually superior to theirs. I just hadn't presented our product in front of the right person. There is some luck involved in getting sales leads and poor leads can leave you high and dry.

I must have gone to over a hundred sales appointments before someone actually decided to buy from me. The weeks prior to that were my first really big test. I could have quit. I could have started looking for other jobs. I could have blamed our product. But for some reason I didn't. I just kept believing in what Tony said and after two months of daily failure, it finally happened: my first sale.

I did it! At approximately 3:30 p.m. on June 22, 1992, I made my first two sales. This is just the beginning of many sales to come (as my sales manager said!). All I have to do is continue to follow the presentation, make improvements when necessary and sustain the strong effort every day. If I keep this up I will realize my goal of $100,000 per year and becoming a sales manager. I feel the power of being in control of my own destiny. It's just a numbers game. As long as I keep getting in front of the right people I will get a proportionate number of sales. Keep it up. This is only the beginning. Use this as a reference to show that hard work does pay off. I learned *during the past two months that it is necessary to fail many times before you succeed. In the past I would have quit long before I made this first sale. Just as I did with the kitchen cutlery sales. Now that I know how to handle failure I will be a major success.*

Eventually I became the top salesperson in the office for three months. I went from making $400 to $1000 per week. Things were certainly looking up. I finally got a refrigerator to replace the ice-cooler. I even got to go to some evening movies. At the very least, I was experiencing some luxuries.

Unfortunately (fortunately, in the big picture), that was not enough for me. I wasn't crazy about what I was doing. I dreaded the thought of Mondays. I didn't feel as though I could do what I wanted when I wanted. I was limited by the job. Even though I now had some money, I didn't seem to have enough vacation days to travel the way I wanted. This growing discontent started to affect my job performance. I went from the number one person in the office to the bottom. My salary, which had increased during my months of high sales volume, was now reduced to where I started. It wasn't the company's fault. My heart just wasn't in it.

I resolved to find a way to have my own business. I just couldn't think of how to do that at the time. Rather than simply quitting, I decided to stick it out. No, it wasn't the job of my dreams, but I needed the money to survive. My focus changed. I spent a good portion of each day thinking of ways I could start my own business. I also tried to learn as much as I could from the business I was currently working in. I started asking a lot of questions about budgeting, marketing, etc. Months passed while I continued in that job. Although I wasn't excited about it, I was excited about the prospect of having my own business in the future.

You know the rest. My parents suggested that I make another attempt at law school. And this time I did not give up. Although I had only about a month to study for the LSAT and was working full time, I did whatever it took to get ready. I took some weekend preparation classes and studied every single night. I don't think I skipped even a day. Now remember, this is the guy who rarely studied in college and thought he could get by on raw intelligence. With this decision, I really had to "gut it out" for the first time in my life. Not only was I working an eight-hour day, I was studying for perhaps five hours per night. On weekends I spent close to ten hours studying. I totally committed myself to doing the best I could on that exam. Even when I took a practice exam and didn't do very well, I just kept at it. The last time I had tried to study for this exam I gave up. I wasn't going to let that happen again. I knew I didn't want to be stuck in my current job. I wanted to improve my situation. In my mind I gave myself no way to bone out this time. I had to make it. I was sick of not living up to my potential and not doing something I really wanted to do. Fortunately, I did well enough to get into law school.

After I finished law school and passed the bar, the next big hurdle was to get my own business started. This is probably the hardest thing I had to do to get myself to where I am today. Trust me, there are so many obstacles you need to overcome to get things running: from getting enough clients to survive to paying your personal bills every month. This is where the rubber meets the road. Tony is not going to be there to help you get these things done. His tapes will help get you motivated to take action, but only you can make it happen.

I started out slowly. The office I rented cost only $300 per month, fully furnished. I managed to obtain most of my office equipment from friends (used) or dirt cheap. With only one client during the first six months of my endeavor, I had to survive on about $1,000 per month. Fortunately, I kept my expenses so low that I was able to pay all my bills on time. Occasionally, some business would come in that would allow me a few luxuries for the month. This situation continued for about a year. But the lack of clients left me feeling as though I wasn't making enough progress.

I decided to partner with an experienced attorney for whom I had worked in law school. Immediately, I was presented with much more legal work, since he had been in business for over 10 years and was quite adept at getting new clients. For a year I learned much about the business of practicing law and obtained some pretty big clients myself. (In Chapter 11, I discuss the importance of role-modeling people who are already good at something.) Things were going well and we were developing a good reputation from the trials we had won. Unfortunately, there came a point where the negative aspects of the partnership outweighed its benefits. We had different long-term goals for the business. I wanted it to give me an opportunity to travel frequently and my need for flexibility with my vacation schedule eventually caused a rift. I wrote extensively in my journal about my frustration with the situation:

My partner does not agree with my big goals for the future. Whenever I talk about us taking many vacations and being able to watch the fort for one another, he gets upset. I didn't go into business for myself to be limited on vacations. I went into business so that I could control my own destiny. I want to be able to go on trips when I want and as much as I want. I don't think that I am asking too much. I'd be perfectly happy if he took as many vacation days as I did. That is part of being partners: to be able to do things better together than we can apart. Although I did just go to Maui (and win Mike's golf tournament!) and Vancouver within the past two weeks, I took a lot of heat for doing so. In fact, my partner even told me that my plane would crash on the way back from Hawaii. That wasn't very nice! We got into a major heated discussion about it when I got back. I don't think this kind of stress is very good. We need to come up with a long-term plan that both of us can live with. Otherwise, I will need to pursue an alternate path.

Later entries in my journal show the stages of my decision to go on my own:

Although it may be difficult to start over, I need to get back to my goal and design my work schedule to be harmonious with my lifestyle. Remember, I went to law school to start my own business so I could control my destiny. Right now I can't do that. I know we are friends, but friends shouldn't stop friends from pursuing their dreams, and that is what is ultimately happening.

I moved my stuff out of our office today. I know that I will be making less money for a while and will have to make some sacrifices, but eventually it will be for the best. I didn't see him changing his long-term goals for our business together. He simply has a different plan and that is okay. I need to pursue my own plan.

This is the beginning of a new era! The Law Offices of Manny Ibay. Everything I have done and endured has taken me to this point. Now is time to use all my experience, education, failures and make it big! Today, I will write out a business plan for the next few months and budget my money. I now have more contacts and legal skills, so I should be able to make it. Go for it!

I made the right decision. I wouldn't have been able to live the lifestyle I have been dreaming about in that situation. As Tony says, I want to be able to do what I want when I want. Now is my time. I went into business for myself so I could have the freedom to work hard, play hard. That is my motto! I need to have fun vacations to look forward to. No one should tell me that I can/cannot go on vacation. I am the one who makes those decisions. I must now set bigger goals and work super hard toward their fulfillment. LET'S DO IT!

Although we went our separate ways, the partnership was mutually beneficial while it lasted and instrumental in my development as an attorney. The following year was quite a struggle. I left the comforts of a nice corner office in downtown Los Angeles and worked out of a spare bedroom in my house. I had to borrow conference rooms and get all new office equipment. I needed to use every dollar I had in reserve to survive those first few months. Despite all the difficulties, I persisted because I knew the lifestyle I wanted and did what was required to get there.

My main point in this chapter is that designing your ideal lifestyle is not going to be easy. In fact, if it is, you should be skeptical about whether you are truly living the life you desire. Even though I followed Tony's books and tapes as closely as possible, I still faced many tough times. Some authors like to leave out the messy details in an effort to show that something can be done. I would rather give you a taste of the difficulties that can arise so that you will not feel alone when they show up for you. Seeing every obstacle I faced not as a problem or reason for quitting but as a challenge to overcome allowed me to design a life where I can do what I want when I want.

9

♦

DON'T EXPECT PERFECTION

One of the biggest mistakes you can make on your way to success is to demand perfection from yourself. By now, I expect that all of you are motivated to go out in the world and kick butt. However, you will set yourself up for failure if you expect to produce a perfect effort every single day for the rest of your life. Your goal should be an outstanding performance every day. And when the day does not go as expected, chalk it up as a bump in the road. It may throw you off course for a little while, but once you get your bearings you'll be able to keep going down that road toward success.

While I was writing an earlier portion of this book I thought I needed to be perfect each and every day. I believed that was an essential qualification for writing a success book. Then one day I just could not get motivated to get things done at the office (even after using all the tricks I discussed in earlier chapters). Since there was nothing that needed to be done immediately, such as prepare a response to a lawsuit, I spent the day doing the minimum work necessary (answering the phone, opening my mail, and sending out bills that were due). I meandered through the day listening to sports radio, calling my friends and checking the internet to see how my stocks were doing.

Obviously, this is not what I would consider an ideally productive day. There was much work on my "to do" list that didn't get done. Does this sound like a day that you have occasionally spent? How often does this happens? Once a month? Every other day?

At first I was extremely disappointed in myself. Was it possible that Tony Robbins or other personal development coaches had days like this? I'm guessing they *have* had a day or two like this. In recalling my experiences over the past ten years, when I went from a job that I hated to doing what I want when I want, I realized that I have had several of these "big loser" days. I realize now that they are bound to occur. The trick is to expect these days to happen from time to time and use them to get you super motivated for the next day. Make a commitment never to have two bad days in a row.

If you know anything about baseball, I'm sure you know that Roger Clemens is a great pitcher. However, there have also been days when this future Hall of Famer could not strike out a little leaguer. During each season, he has had several outings when he was just plain bad. However, if you really know your stats, you'll notice that he usually bounces back from a terrible game with an outstanding pitching performance. That is what you need to do in your daily life. Yes, you will have those bad outings. I sure do. I'm sure that Tony does too. Making a conscious effort to bounce back the next day with an outstanding effort is what makes the difference between an average pitcher and a future Hall of Famer.

And that is also the difference between an average working stiff and someone who has what he or she wants in life.

Dealing With Bad Days

We all know when we haven't been at our best. If I am honest with myself, I can tell you at the end of every day whether I put forth the proper effort. When you've had a sub-par day, acknowledge it to yourself. But also understand that this is part of life and accept it. Don't put yourself in a worse state by telling yourself that you're a big loser. You may have been a loser today, but not in the grand scheme of things. Life is a long race. What matters is not whether you had a bad day or two, but that you're able to create enough good days to get you where you want to go.

After you acknowledged a bad day, isolate exactly what you should have done instead. In my case, I know that I should have finished everything on my to-do list so I can move on to some new business. I was merely putting off my work for another time (since I knew it wasn't urgent). Now that I knew what the problem was, I could start the next day focused on making sure that would not happen again – at least not on consecutive days. We usually know deep down what is necessary to get what we want. The high school student knows when he has studied enough to get the grades he wants. The parent knows whether or not he has spent enough time with his kids to establish the type of relationship he wants. The professional golfer knows if he has practiced hitting his driver enough to play a particular course and get the score he wants. And the lawyer knows if he has prepared his closing argument well enough to persuade a jury that his client is innocent.

Although we cannot know exactly how our efforts will turn out, we can certainly make an educated guess. I may not have known exactly how well I would score on the bar exam, but I knew that, based on my preparation, I would do well enough to pass. (I actually passed two bar exams – California and Nevada – on the first try!)

I think a lot of people pretend not to know whether they are making their best effort. It is easy to think you are doing okay. You need to scrutinize your day. You need to be able to tell yourself whether or not you did your best.

Benjamin Franklin graded his efforts on a regular basis. He went even further: he graded himself on twelve "virtues" to determine how he was doing in each category. He knew what he did well and what needed improvement. He did this on a daily basis. The problem with most of us is that we don't want to know when something is going wrong, for fear it will cause us stress. However, once you begin evaluating yourself on a daily basis, you will see that it is not stressful. Quite the contrary, in fact.

Since I have implemented my daily self-evaluation I am much more relaxed. I know each and every day whether I am getting closer to my goals. It is comforting and encouraging to know you are making progress.

(By the way, the reason I started reading Benjamin Franklin's autobiography was that Tony said he read the book. If you want to be successful, read the books that successful people read.)

During the past year, I have begun to write down on my calendar certain symbols that indicate the type of day I had. I put the letter "O" on days I believe that I am outstanding in all areas of my life, i.e., relationship, physical fitness, time management, and productivity. I put the letter "L" when I have a loser day. (I leave a blank space for mediocre days.) You would not believe what a great tool this can be to keep you performing at your best. Sometimes during a particular day, I can feel myself slipping from being outstanding to being mediocre. When I think about having a day without the "O" written down, I tell myself: Don't slack off. You want to be outstanding today. And most of the time it works. People like to see they are getting good grades. Even adults. I want my calendar to be filled with "O's."

Rewarding Outstanding Performance

I got this idea one Christmas when I went to see my fiancée's parents and siblings in Buffalo. In every family member's household, I saw a chart on the refrigerator, which was placed there on St. Nicholas Day (December 6). Every child had a box next to their name for each day from St. Nicholas Day until Christmas. The kids are told that if they get all stars (actual sticker stars) Santa will be good to them this year. The rule is that you get a star if you had an outstanding (well-behaved) day. Sometimes they got double stars for exceptional days. On the flip side, they got a black mark for days they were not well-behaved. Boy, did those kids hate black marks. In fact, it was generally big news throughout the whole family (there are seven brothers and sisters) when someone got a black mark. Usually there were only one or two black marks for all nine grandchildren during each Christmas season. And you know what, it works. The kids were always on their best behavior during this period of "evaluation" that was going to be presented to Santa Claus.

I thought they should have something like this for the whole year. I mean, if it got the kids to perform at their very best, why not implement something similar during the "off-season" and use different rewards? These could be toys they would have gotten anyway during the year. Or movie tickets. Or a trip to Disneyland after an excellent month.

Then it hit me. Why not start a daily evaluation chart of my own to help me perform at my very best? It was easy to come up with my rewards. They did not have to be something major every week, but they at least provided something to shoot for. I started rewarding myself with a nice dinner (Spago), theater tickets or Tony's latest CD program. But I got those rewards only when I had an outstanding week. I did not get a reward if there was a "black mark" on my calendar. The most important thing about this chart was that it got me to do an honest evaluation of my performance on that particular day. Not every day received a "star." But many of them did. And I was able to give myself many rewards. I figured that I made more than enough extra money during those "outstanding" weeks to cover the additional expenses.

This might sound silly to you. But it works. Try it out for a month. How do you conduct yourself when your performance is being evaluated by someone other than your boss? Be honest with your evaluations. You know your potential. Did you work at your full potential today? If so, give yourself a star and try to keep this up for an entire week. If you get all stars this week, reward yourself with something you normally don't get to have. Remember, just like my nieces and nephews during the Christmas season, we all need something to shoot for.

10

$\blacklozenge$

HOW MASSIVE FAILURE EQUALS SUCCESS

I know what you are thinking. The title of this chapter doesn't seem to make any sense. How can massive failure equal success? I was always trained to believe that massive failure equals ... well, massive failure.

Fortunately, Tony helped me see that massive failure actually does equal success. You're wondering: how could that be? Tony makes it seem simple: the bigger the goal, the more failure you will need to endure in order to reach "success." For instance, let's say that you want to sell a piece of commercial real estate (which I did for a while). For someone starting out in the business, the only way to develop a clientele of buyers and sellers is to make the dreaded cold-calls. Everyone hates doing that, but it is a necessity unless you happen to be related to a group of property owners. The process is arduous. On the average, it may take a hundred phone calls to reach someone interested in hearing what you have to say. It may take a thousand calls to actually make a sale. That means that on the average, you are failing 999 times out of 1000 (massive failure).

How would you feel about experiencing that on a daily basis? It sounds terribly painful. However, the rewards can be great. That one sale might result in a six-figure commission. Two or three times more than you could make at a regular job, where you need not "fail" 99.9 percent of the time. That's why those individuals make so much money when they succeed. The greater amount of failure associated with a task, the greater the rewards. Those who are able to succeed in this environment understand that massive failure actually equals success. Think about everyone you know who is doing extremely well. I'm willing to bet they had to go through a process where many of their contemporaries had given up because they could not handle massive failure.

A great example of this premise can be found in the history books. Thomas Edison "failed" about 10,000 times before he developed the electric light bulb. However, he never considered these attempts to be "failures." He always said to himself and to others that this "failure" was actually a "discovery," of one more way the light bulb would not work. Fortunately, he believed deep down, that massive failure would ultimately lead to success. Otherwise, we might still be living like Charles and Laura Ingalls on *Little House on the Prairie*. Without that strong conviction, it would have been easy to give up after the 100th or 1000th failed attempt.

I'm sure you've heard about Sylvester Stallone. He got rejected by every agent in New York several times before he finally got someone interested in buying the *Rocky* script. He faced even more rejection when he refused to sell the script without having the opportunity to star in the movie himself. He experienced massive failure before he hit the big time. One of the best stories I heard Tony tell was of his conversation with Stallone.

Immediately prior to *Rocky*, Sly was at rock bottom. Probably lower than any of us have ever gotten. He had sold all of his possessions just to pay for rent and food while shopping his *Rocky* script. His wife checked out of the picture after he sold her jewelry. All he had was his dog. Then, something amazing happened. Someone wanted to buy his script. In fact, they were willing to pay $250,000. But there was one condition. He would not be allowed to star in the movie. Sly knew that his destiny was to be a famous actor as well as a writer. With less than $500 to his name, he rejected the $250,000. How many of us could have done that? Not me.

As the story continued things got even worse for Sly. He said the lowest moment in his life came when he had to sell his dog for $25, just to survive. The dog that was his best (and only) friend in the world. Just when all seemed lost, the producers called back and agreed to buy his script, even with him starring in it. The rest is movie history. Not only did he become one of the top box-office stars of all time, *Rocky* won the Best Picture Oscar in 1976.

But that's not the end of the story! After getting $35,000 for his script and a percentage of the profits, (he took a cut from the original $250,000 in exchange for playing the starring role) he went looking for his best friend. Sly offered the new owner $100 to get his dog back. The owner refused. $500....NO! $1,000....NO! Sly paid $15,000 just to get his dog back and gave that person a part in the *Rocky* movie. As for his best friend, well, you remember Butkus (the dog in *Rocky*).

If Sylvester Stallone had believed that massive failure and

rejection meant he was a loser, it's unlikely we would have ever had the pleasure to see any of the *Rocky* or *Rambo* movies. The same is true for many of today's "success stories." Michael Jordan failed to make his high school basketball team. Even our man Tony Robbins was $758,000 in debt and on the verge of bankruptcy before he turned it around to give us *Personal Power*.

I'd like to end this section by telling you about the biggest "failure" of them all. In 1831, this man failed in business. In 1832, he ran for state legislator and lost. In 1833, he attempted to go into business again and it failed. In 1835, his fiancée died. He had a nervous breakdown in 1836. In 1843, he ran for Congress and was defeated. In 1848, he tried again to run for Congress and lost. In 1855, he ran for the Senate and lost. The following year he ran for Vice President and lost again.

The good news is that *he did not give up*. In 1860, this person, who had experienced massive failure, was elected the sixteenth President of the United States. His name: Abraham Lincoln.

Think about the last time you tried something, failed at it several times and gave up. The first time I became involved in the sales field was back in college. I went to one of those "quick money" events where they showed us how we could make a lot of money selling kitchen cutlery (a fancy name for knives). We got to hear some of the top salesman talk about their "success stories" and how much money they were making. It was all tremendously exciting. Then came the hard part – actually going out and selling. First, we had to pay about $100 for our sales kit, a lot of money back in 1983. So off I went. I was enthusiastic for the first couple of presentations. However, nobody bought even a single knife. All I had to show for my efforts was a bunch of rejections. This was the first time I had experienced such negative feedback. Within a week, I decided that I couldn't do this. It must be a scam. So I gave up. I stayed away from selling for a long time after that.

Next I looked for employment that would involve less rejection. A job where I could simply perform a task and get paid for it. Something that did not involve "selling" and "rejection." Jobs in the clerical, administrative and accounting fields. I did this for a couple of years. I earned respectable money, but far from anything exciting. I worked at typical 9 to 5 jobs where I would expect to get a raise every six months or so. However, after laboring in mediocrity for some time, I realized that the only people who were really making it were those running their own business, or those who brought business to their company, the so-called rainmakers.

The one job I had that particularly exemplifies this principle was as a loan representative, trying to persuade people to refinance their homes. Trust me, it is extremely difficult to call someone at 8:00 p.m. on a Tuesday night and get them to talk to you. I'm sure you've had your share of experiences with over-zealous telemarketers. However, the payoff was relatively big for me at the time. My previous job had paid about $10 per hour. With this new job, I could make $500 – $1,000 for each refinance. At first, it was extremely frustrating. People would hang up on me. They would curse at me. I got about seventy-five "no's" or hang-ups before I actually got to speak to someone for longer than 15 seconds. Fortunately, secure in Tony's principle, I did not give up. Rather than going home thinking I was a total failure, I kept telling myself: "Massive failure equals success." Unless you get a rare lucky break, you will need to fail massively before you reach any type of success. I think I went a couple of months before making my first sale. It did not make me rich financially, but I finally realized that Tony's statement was true. If you want to make more money than the average guy, you really need to cultivate perseverance in the face of massive failure.

Fortunately, I was able to pull myself from rock bottom with the additional money coming in. But even though I was making more money, I was still experiencing rejection and failure 99 percent of the time. What Tony's new concept taught me was that I needed to get through the 99 "no's" before I could get to that one person who would say yes. For someone without the right beliefs, it is easy to give up before ever reaching the first sale. I recall that I started with over ten new people. After a couple of weeks, there were only two of us left. And neither of us had made a sale by that time. Luckily, we truly believed that we needed to fail massively before we would get to taste success.

This principle is true in all areas of life, not just in sales. Tony likes to use the example of an average baby. How many times do you think he or she falls down and "fails" while trying to walk for the first time? Quite a few. What would happen if babies simply gave up? There would be many adults out there walking on all fours. Fortunately, babies are too young to be "psyched out" by their failures. The sad part is that we learn to fear our failures sometime between infancy and our teenage years. How many of you were terrified to ask for your first date? Remember how scared you were that you would be rejected? Probably the best advice we can give our kids is to teach them that massive failure equals success. In practical terms this translates to:

- Ask out as many girls/guys as possible so you will lose that fear of rejection. Who cares if he or she says no.

After you've been rejected once, it gets a lot easier.

- Keep trying to hit that golf ball or baseball, no matter how many times you miss. Babe Ruth struck out more times than anyone else. The only chance you have to be as good as Tiger Woods is if you "fail" as much as he did. Do you think he always hit the ball as well as he does now? He must have hit many terrible shots in his youth to develop the game he has today. You have to fail many times before you can eventually succeed.

- The time to study harder is when you are failing to get the grades that you need to get into college. Many students tend to give up after getting bad grades because they don't want to be disappointed. Successful students are the ones who can use their "disappointments" to their advantage.

I think the worst thing that can happen when you are young is for success to come too easily. Remember all the "cool" people in high school, the popular ones with the nice cars and clothes? The ones who were given everything and did not have to work a lick. Many of them just couldn't handle life in the real world. They couldn't handle failures and not looking good. Those of you who weren't handed everything on a silver platter, be happy about it. You've had to work (and fail along the way) for everything. Be proud of that. What I noticed at my high school reunion was that many of the "geeks" turned out to be the biggest successes, both socially and financially. They are examples of how massive failure (in high school/college) can actually give us a better chance at ultimate success. It is likely that in their "difficult" teenage years they learned how to handle failure and adversity, which allowed them to succeed much later.

Speaking of adversity, let me tell you about the week I just had. During these last couple of days I have experienced two huge "failures." I just lost a high-profile case that was reported in the newspapers. In addition, a big real estate deal fell through and I lost my commission. That is a lot to take without the right mind-set. Fortunately, with Tony's belief ingrained in my mind over the past ten years I was able to take these setbacks in stride. I told myself, once again: *Massive failure will lead to ultimate success.*

And I really believe it. I know that in order to close that big sale I've got to lose several others. I know that even if I lose a trial, the experience I gain will add to my skills and increase my chances of success in the future. (Of course, there are some cases that are un-winnable, no matter how great a lawyer you are.)

This is how you must think if you want to achieve really big successes in life. One last hint: if you are not experiencing failure on a regular basis, you are probably doing something that doesn't have a big pay-off. Remember, even Tiger Woods experiences failure (not winning) more often than success.

Here's an excerpt from my success journal that sums up my thoughts on this important subject:

> *I started listening to a new set of Tony's CD's entitled "Get the Edge." In it he discusses how all problems/ resistance I experience strengthen my mental muscles. Without resistance you don't grow. It's that simple. You should welcome resistance when it comes so that you can grow stronger than you are. Remember, we don't grow/improve when we play against somebody that we can easily beat. I recall one of the best rounds of golf I*

ever played was against a 2-handicap golfer. I actually played at his level. Compare this to the times I played against people who were mediocre golfers. I played down to their level because there was no incentive to do well. I could win easily by playing average golf. Welcome resistance (failure) because it will take you to the next level.

11

ROLE MODELING

Tony taught me that "role modeling," (imitating the actions and beliefs of successful people), will greatly speed up the process of getting what you want. In *Personal Power*, Tony talks about his own use of role modeling in his early days. When he was thirty-eight pounds overweight he looked for someone who had started from a similar position. An individual who had been able to lose all his excess weight and keep it off. Tony patterned his actions on what he learned from this successful person, and he has kept his body looking good ever since. He did the same in the area of relationships. He found a man who had married the woman of his dreams and asked him a series of questions:

1) How did you manage to attract her?
2) What do you do to keep your relationship at this high level?

The point here is, why try to re-invent the wheel? If your goal is something that someone has already accomplished, find out what that person did to accomplish that goal. The easiest way to do this is by reading biographies or how-to books by people who have accomplished the goals you desire. Of course, the best approach would be to address a series of questions directly to the successful person.

We see this principle used in the workplace all the time. When a new employee starts a particular job, he is usually partnered with a more experienced person who can show him the ropes. For instance, in the sales field, new reps often "ride along" with veteran reps to watch how they give their presentations. This allows them not only to learn the right sales pitch but also to observe the nuances of this kind of exchange.

Unfortunately, people rarely use role modeling when it comes to non-work-related goals. If you are interested in getting in shape, don't rely only on your own knowledge. There is so much information in the areas of nutrition, aerobic/weight training, and the right mental approach to losing weight that it would be foolish to try to figure it all out on your own. Get a personal trainer. You'd be surprised how many people spend a great deal of time at the gym doing what they think is right, only to find out later that they were wasting their efforts.

The same is true in relationships. So many couples are unhappy and can't seem to figure out what to do about it. If neither person has been in a successful relationship before, how could they possibly have the know-how to build a quality situation for themselves?

I am not saying that you need to go to a marriage counselor for every little conflict. However, it would be helpful to consult with couples who seem to be experiencing satisfying relationships. (Guys, there is nothing wrong with reading a John Gray book!)

Isn't it interesting that kids from happy families (with parents who have loving relationships) tend to have happy families themselves. The reason is simple. They were able to observe what made things work between their parents. The opposite tends to be true as well. Children with unhappily married parents never get to see what it takes to develop a quality relationship. As Tony says, don't underestimate the *power of role modeling*. It can save you a lot of time and trouble.

One of the best things I did when I started my law practice was to have serious, in depth, question-and-answer sessions with lawyers who had successfully operated their own businesses for over twenty years. These people knew what worked and what didn't. They knew what obstacles I would face and could tell me in advance how to handle them. I can't tell you how valuable these conversations have been to the success of my business. I didn't have to re-invent the wheel. When you undertake something as serious as starting your own business, you don't want to waste time and money learning by trial and error. I asked questions about how much space to lease, when you need to get an assistant, what type of computer equipment to buy, where to get the best/cheapest business cards, how to get clients, etc. Not only did I get answers to these basic questions, I was able to watch and observe how these seasoned lawyers spoke to prospective clients, how they conducted themselves in social settings, what restaurants they went to, how they ordered dinner, how they dressed, when they were serious and when they were light-hearted. Furthermore, by hanging around with such distinguished attorneys, I felt less intimidated when I went up against them in the courtroom. So don't re-invent the wheel, role model. And if you want to be successful, role model the best.

◆ Assignment ◆

Area you want to improve   Role Model

_____   _____

_____   _____

_____   _____

12

◆

NO MORE IDENTITY CRISIS

Prior to listening to Tony Robbins, I never really focused on my "identity." It was just something I didn't give much thought to. However, I have realized that having the proper identity is an extremely powerful tool in getting ourselves to make the changes we want and to take the appropriate action. I also realized that in the past my sense of who I was held me back.

In high school, I believed that I was a "geek" and a "loser." I didn't think any girl would want to go out with me, let alone talk to me. This picture I had of myself stuck with me all through high school and limited my actions. I never dared approach any of the girls I liked because my identity was not compatible with that action. Even when I had what looked like a great opportunity to speak to a girl, I opted not to because of my identity as a "geek." Many teenagers act this way, and the important thing is to understand why. I believed deep down that no one would be interested in me.

Fortunately, this identity changed when I got to college.

Sometimes it takes something unexpected to break your pattern and change your belief about yourself. I well remember that day I made my own breakthrough. I was walking to class and found a penny. I picked it up and thought this is a sign that good things are going to happen. While I was standing in line buying dinner that night, a girl I especially liked started talking to me. I couldn't believe it! When the initial shock wore off, I had my first real conversation with a female and we sat down to have dinner together. We then went to a review class where we sat next to each other. This pattern continued for several weeks. All of a sudden, her friends were talking to me and I started to feel confident enough to talk to them. My identity was changing. I no longer considered myself a loser who was too scared to talk to girls. I was actually beginning to think of myself as popular. I started going to parties, meeting more and more people. I started to take care in choosing the clothes I wore every day. I wouldn't wear anything that wouldn't fit with my "cool" image. It turned out that being popular was not a problem for me in college. I was even voted "Stud of the Month" in my dorm. I'm proud of that, not because of the silly title, but because it confirmed how much I had changed since high school.

Of course, all this happened before I started the Tony Robbins program. I tell that story because it illustrates the power of identity. Nothing about me changed much between high school and college. I didn't get major cosmetic surgery, win the lottery or get muscular all of a sudden. All that changed was merely my sense of myself.

———————◆———————

Recognizing The Limitations of Your Present Self-Image

My problem in 1991 was also an identity problem: I believed I was a loser in terms of money and success. That's when Tony's lessons on identity really helped. After Tony convinced me of the need to expand my identity, I used some of the exercises in *Awaken the Giant Within* to help me reinvent myself.

At the time, I considered myself to be this way:

I Am...
- *A relatively laid-back person who doesn't want to work too hard.*
- *Someone who doesn't like anyone telling him what to do.*
- *Someone who doesn't know what he wants to do with the rest of his life.*
- *Someone who doesn't like to plan for the future.*
- *Someone who does things only when he feels like it.*

I'm sure you can guess that this identity did not take me very far in life. I expected that things would come to me easily; if they didn't, I was unwilling to exert any extra effort toward getting them. This was my identity, and until I changed it there was no chance I would become successful.

After hearing Tony talk about identity, I finally realized that the only way of changing my actions was to change my belief about who I was. Let me give you some examples of how my previous identity did the most damage:

Whenever my job became more difficult and required more

time and effort, I decided it was not "right" for me. I wanted a high-paying job that demanded minimal effort on my part. Which is probably why I had sixteen different jobs in the first four years out of college. I did not want to be the "hard-working nerd," at the company. I believed it was beneath me to have to work so hard. I wanted to get by on my natural talent and ability. I believed I shouldn't have to work as hard as other employees who weren't as smart. (Sometimes being smarter than others works to your disadvantage if you believe you no longer have to try as hard.) Bottom line: I was never able to succeed in a single job with this attitude and "identity."

At school I had the same I-don't-need-to-work-that-hard mentality. It wasn't "me" to study so hard. It wasn't good for my reputation as a laid-back person. As a result, I never did as well as I could have done. It was only after I followed Tony's ideas about identity that I was able to achieve academic success in law school.

Obviously, it would be difficult to become successful at anything with my previous "identity." In Tony's recent CD program *Lessons in Mastery*, he included the section about identity on disk one. I can see why he decided to emphasize this. Nothing will change unless you change your identity first.

The most difficult step for me was to shed the I-don't-need-to-work-hard image. When you live many years believing yourself to be a certain way it takes major effort to change. Immersing myself with Tony's books and tapes helped me overcome this big hurdle. I finally got it through my thick skull that no one ever becomes truly successful without working at it. Of course, my parents had been telling me that for years, but I never listened to them. I have since come to realize that most of the things they told me to do were correct.

Envisioning Your New Identity

Using my success journal, I wrote down the type of person I wanted (and needed) to become.

My new identity

> *I am a hard-working, self disciplined person who now knows that it will take much effort to become truly successful. Since I was lazy for so many years, I will need to work harder than everyone else so I can overtake my peers.*

This was a significant start. Through my new identity, I was able to do things that I was never able to accomplish before. I finally put forth my best effort on things I was working on. Prior to that, I was always content to say, "I didn't study too hard for the exam, but I could have done better if I'd really wanted to." Once I jettisoned my previous identity, everything became easier. I was able to study as hard as possible for a test and feel good about it, even on the rare occasions when I did not do as well as I had hoped. My work habits also improved dramatically. I no longer had to prove to everyone that I was Mr. Laid-Back, so I was able to start kicking some butt. It was not until I changed this identity that I was able to stay on a job for longer than eleven months (my record prior to *Personal Power*).

I really noticed this change when I began law school. I now told myself, and anyone who asked – "*Nobody works harder than me during finals week.*" The same attitude helped me sail through the bar exam. I believed that no one worked harder than I did. When potential fun distractions came up, I always fell back on my identity to make the appropriate decision.

I began to describe myself as a "work hard/play hard" person. The new identity was solidly in place now. Yes, I worked super hard, but nobody had more fun than I did either. Over the years, I have improved upon my identity statement even further. As you will read in the next chapter, I used Tony's life management program to establish a purposeful identity in all areas of my life.

Right now, the best thing you can do for yourself is to honestly write a description of your current identity:

✦ My Identity Today ✦

Will this "identity," get you to where you want to go in life? If not, write down the way you want to be identified in the future:

✦ My New Identity ✦

Trust me, until your identity becomes congruent with your goals, you will never be truly successful.

13

◆

THE TIME OF MY LIFE: RESULTS MANAGEMENT

My favorite Tony Robbins CD program is called *The Time of Your Life*. It focuses on planning your life and is quite an improvement on traditional time management systems that revolve around a to-do list. Tony emphasizes that in today's fast-paced society, it is no longer optimal to manage your life using a to-do list. In this program, he stresses the importance of knowing your outcomes (daily, weekly, monthly, yearly) and exactly why you want to achieve each one. Once you know your desired outcome and why you want to achieve it, the final step is to design your action plan. Tony's acronym OPA stands for Outcome focused, Purpose driven, Action plan.

I began using this system approximately eight years after I completed *Personal Power*. I was beginning to get extremely busy at work and wanted a better way to manage my affairs. At the time, I was using a conventional to-do list. Unfortunately, things kept piling up and I was not satisfied with what was getting accomplished.

The concept of understanding why you want to achieve your goals was not unfamiliar to me, since Tony discusses it in great detail in his *Personal Power* program as well as in *Awaken the Giant Within*. However, I applied these techniques only when writing about my major goals in life. I did not realize the benefits of applying the process on a daily or weekly basis.

My previous time management system consisted of making a list of all the things I needed to do. In my law practice alone, that list usually included 70 to 80 items. When I added tasks that needed to be done at home, it could tally over 100 items. I credit *The Time of Your Life* program with saving my sanity in this frustrating situation. In this program, Tony offers a variety of techniques that helped me get a better handle on the time factor in my life. I now realize I was operating at only 20 percent of my capability because I was managing my time so inefficiently. Most of the time, I was not doing the things that could actually make a difference in my life or business. In fact, I was not spending time on things I really wanted out of life.

Tony discusses what he calls "time targets" and classifies all activities into four categories:

1) The Dimension of Distraction – activities that are not important and not urgent.
2) The Dimension of Delusion – activities that are urgent but not important.
3) The Dimension of Demand – activities that are urgent and important.
4) The Zone – activities that are very important, but not urgent.

The realization that all activities fall into one of these

classifications got me excited about the program. When you start isolating how much time you spend in each of these areas, you can determine whether you are managing the time of your life properly.

Classifying Your Activities

In the workbook that accompanies the program I wrote down the following activities for each category. See how my list compares to yours.

Dimension of Distraction
1) *Surfing the internet, reading every article in ESPN.com, checking my stocks every 10 minutes.*
2) *Listening to Sports Radio, e.g., Jim Rome, Loony & Dave, Arnie Spanier, Kylie & Booms.*
3) *Watching television shows I am really not interested in.*

Dimension of Delusion
1) *Answering every phone call that comes in.*
2) *Reading and responding to all my emails as they come in.*

Dimension of Demand
1) *Preparing legal documents that are behind schedule or need to be completed ASAP.*
2) *Handling my spouse after she has a very bad day at work.*
3) *Having relatives in town.*
4) *Early morning court appearances.*

The Zone
1) *Writing in my success journal.*
2) *Reading a Tony Robbins/success book.*
3) *Running/Lifting Weights.*
4) *Doing things to get ahead of schedule at work.*
5) *Planning my future.*
6) *Going to a Tony Robbins Seminar.*

I discovered that I need to spend as much time as possible in The Zone. In the workbook, Tony asks you to write down all the things you would like to do if you had a couple of extra hours per week. I believe that exercise was instrumental in giving me the ability to write this book and accomplish many other things that were once on my wish list. In March 2000, I wrote down the following activities I wanted to spend more time doing:

1) *Learn how to be a better trial lawyer by reading books, watching trials and going to seminars.*
2) *Learn how to be a better person and spend more time in the zone.*
3) *More quality time with my girl doing new/fun things which will increase the level of our relationship.*
4) *Exercise every day – running, walking, lifting weights.*
5) *Writing my book.*
6) *Making more contacts to increase business which will lead to more $$.*
7) *Time to improve relationships with relatives and friends.*
8) *Working on cases/projects that increase my knowledge/value.*
9) *Learn to speak French so I can live in Paris for several months at a time.*

I noticed when I was spending most of time in The Zone I was feeling more fulfilled and less stressed. In the beginning, I spent only about 10 to 20 percent of my time in The Zone. Now I spend about 50 percent. You would be amazed what a difference this has made in my life. I have not eliminated the time spent doing urgent and important things, but through preparation I have been able to reduce the number of last-minute rush jobs which I handle. When you are spending only a small percentage of your time putting out fires, it does not drain you the way it would if you were doing it most of the time. In fact, once you are spending most of your time in The Zone, it is refreshing to work on a project with a deadline, since it challenges you to go beyond your normal limits.

Creating Your Life Plan

Once I had a better understanding of how I spent my time, I was able to proceed further with the program. The next major area Tony focuses on is creating your life plan. Not just writing down random goals you would like to achieve, but detailing what you would like to accomplish in every category of your life – personal as well as professional. Doing this enabled me to establish greater balance in my life. Many people are outstanding in one area, such as their career or their physical body, but overlook other important areas such as relationships and family. Tony teaches you that doing well in all areas of your life is total success. What's the value of being a millionaire, if your body is falling apart and your relationship with your spouse is in shambles? I thought I was doing pretty well before *The Time of*

Your Life, but this program allowed me to expand my focus to include all the important areas in my life.

Finding What Needs Improvement

The first step was to determine my categories of improvement, in both my professional and personal life. Then I was instructed to write down a description of my vision for success in each category. I came up with the following list:

CATEGORIES OF IMPROVEMENT – PERSONAL

I. *PHYSICAL STRENGTH AND ENERGY*
   To be Superman, with unlimited energy from running at least 3x/week, who eats the right food in the right amount and is working out with weights to look better than Bruce (Lee) and to be the Sexiest Man Alive. (You have to be outrageous and playful, as Tony says.)

II. *EMOTIONAL MASTERY*
   To focus on what is great, to spend little time focusing on things I can't control or stupid people. To be in control of my emotions and to maximize my life.

III. *EXCITING RELATIONSHIP*
   To be a great, exciting fiancée who is trying to improve an already amazing relationship. To develop a mutual relationship to help each other be the best we can be.

IV. *GREAT FRIENDSHIPS/FAMILY RELATIONSHIPS*
   To have many friends I can have fun with, who can enrich my life with their ideas/motivation. To be able to

help my friends through my life experience. To have a close bond with my family and try to improve our already great relationships.

V. FINANCIAL FREEDOM

To be able to do what I want when I want and as much as I want. To be a multi-millionaire who has everything I could possibly want: a house in Bel Air, a Ferrari Spyder, first class vacations, and the ability to provide completely for my family.

VI. CONSTANT AND NEVER ENDING IMPROVEMENT

To be striving for continuous and never ending improvement in all categories even when I have already made lots of money & experienced much success. Success must always be improved upon for lifetime success. Consistent persistence: think like TIGER!

VII. PERSONAL PEAK PERFORMANCE

I will strive to always improve my skills via books, tapes, seminars and life experience. That is how I got this far and that is what will eventually lead to lifetime success.

CATEGORIES OF IMPROVEMENT - PROFESSIONAL

I. TRIAL LAWYER

I want to be a big-time trial lawyer who is sought after for million-dollar cases. I will continuously improve my skills by reading books, watching trials, and going to seminars.

II. SALESMAN

I am a rainmaker who gets plenty of new business. I have an amazing personality and people like me.

I know that I need to consistently market my legal services in order to get as many referrals as possible. I will attempt to learn as much as possible about legal marketing so I can afford all the things I desire.

III. *BUSINESS MANAGER*

I plan ahead and budget my income and expenses for at least 90 days. This will enable me to continue to be in business for myself and continue to grow to be a big time trial lawyer. I never want to work for someone else!

IV. *OUTSTANDING SUPPORT OF EXISTING CLIENTS*

I am a time-efficient productive worker who does his best for clients in a timely & thorough manner. I know that I will continue to grow by having ecstatic clients. I strive to be Outstanding!

V. *AUTHOR*

I will be a famous, best-selling author as long as I know what I want, think about it daily, and take massive action. I have much life experience in personal development since I've had the great fortune of hitting rock bottom and getting back to the top.

I wrote this list after finishing Tony's *The Time of Your Life* program and have been updating it regularly. It paints a clear picture of where I want to go in each important area of my life. I am undoubtedly way ahead of where I would have been with my old time management techniques. Tony has taught me *life management* with this program which I highly recommend. One great feature of his programs is that they all come with a money back guarantee. That means you can listen to them for thirty days and still return them for any reason. When I first saw this offer I thought I might just buy it, listen to it, and then return it. However, it was so good, and I wrote so many great things in the workbook, it never crossed my mind to send it back. Trust me, if you apply his stuff to its full potential you can be millions ahead (as some people at his seminar have attested to).

Shaping Your Ultimate Life Vision and Purpose

To complete my vision for success, I wrote down my life's ultimate vision and ultimate purpose. This was a synopsis of all the categories, which I reviewed on a daily basis. Doing this enabled me to wake up every day and know what I was going for and why. It creates incredible motivation and momentum to begin each morning. I'm sure you have experienced days like this in the past. Tony helps you have more of these days through seeing your desires clearly set down on paper.

My Life's Ultimate Vision

I want to be a super-successful, electrifying trial lawyer who has the skills to win/get the big money cases. I want to be The Rainmaker, the ultimate sweet talking salesman who gets an unlimited amount of quality business. I want to be the best fiancée in the entire world, who is constantly trying to improve his relationship and do his best to take care of his girl. I want to be the most fun, energetic person, life of the party; the person everyone is dying to be around. I want to be the best possible son/relative who values and makes the most of all of the time he has available to spend with his family.

I want to be the ultimate motivator, teacher and writer who has the accomplishments, skills and knowledge to help others reach their potential. I want to be the Sexiest Man Alive, the most energetic person in the entire world.

My Life's Ultimate Purpose
To be able to do what I want when I want and as much as I want! To be known as someone who has made it Big, walks his talk, and is outstanding in what he does – à la T. Woods. To be able to take care of my family and provide them with everything they need to be happy and successful in their own right. To know that I made the most of my enormous potential. To create the healthiest, best looking body I can, which will give me the strength, vitality and confidence to exceed all of my goals.

The best part about buying Tony's CD program was the ability to go back and review what I learned. It's important to remember, when implementing new concepts and strategies to improve your life, that they will take some time to become part of you. Just listening to the program once, doesn't make you a master at managing your life. Not only did I have to listen to it several times, I had to consciously use what I learned on a daily basis.

Trouble Shooting With OPA

I recently got myself in a little bit of a rut at work. Although other areas of my life were going really well – I was exercising like a madman, having a great relationship with my fiancée, and doing an excellent job with my book – I noticed that I was not totally motivated at my law office. I was feeling pretty blasé and not performing to my full potential. Despite the fact that I was evaluating my performance on a daily basis, I still felt that I could do a lot more.

That is when I decided to go back and review Tony's program one more time. This helped me see that the reason I was doing well in all other areas of my life, yet slacking off at the office, was that I did not have clear outcomes in mind with exciting reasons behind them. Even when you have your own business, things can get pretty mundane.

So I went back to the basic premise of the OPA program. I had to figure out what type of exciting outcome I needed to get me back to performing at 100 percent. Did I want to make more money? Yes. But would that alone get me motivated every day, each and every hour. Not really. Deep down, I felt that I was making enough money to do the things I wanted, so the idea of making more was not enough to do the trick. I knew that without a clear outcome, I would not perform at my optimum levels. I struggled with this question for several weeks. What outcome would get me really juiced?

After some serious brainstorming, I realized that the one outcome/goal that got me excited was having a longer weekend. At the time, I was working a typical five-day week even though I could easily have done all my work in three or four days. I said to myself: Why don't I just work super hard for three or four days and get all my work done, so I can have a long weekend almost every week? That turned out to be the million-dollar question. All of a sudden, I had this super-exciting outcome I could shoot for every week. Naturally, there were some weeks when there was no way I could finish everything in three days. Sometimes, especially during a trial, I ended up working all seven days and had no weekend. But the best part was knowing there was a chance of having a long weekend every week. I increased my excitement by writing down what would be great about having a three- or four-day weekend:

1) *Having the ability to go out and have fun on a Monday or Tuesday with the knowledge that most people are working.*

2) *Playing golf on weekdays when there are fewer people on the course.*

3) *Having more time to spend on my book and working out.*

4) *Having more time to recharge every week so I can really put forth a great effort during the 3 or 4 days I do work. (I actually think I am making more money working less time because I really give it 110 percent.)*

5) *Most importantly, the time to take long weekend trips to Carmel or Santa Barbara – my favorite spots for wine tasting.*

(I also purchased *The Time of Your Life* program for a friend who always seems to be living in the Dimension of Demand.) It has helped me take my life to another level, one where I am successful in all categories of my life.

You don't need your own business to use the OPA system. It is something you can apply toward everything you do. You can even use it to plan a great weekend.

14

$\blacklozenge$

CONSTANT AND NEVER ENDING IMPROVEMENT

Once you reach some measure of success, there is a point where you can become complacent. For instance, if your goal is to lose twenty-five pounds and you have managed to lose fifteen, your desire to lose that additional ten may not be as strong as when you first started. Or, when your goal is to have your own business, and it has been operating for two or three years at a respectable profit, you may be less determined to go that extra mile to seek additional sources of revenue.

That was the situation I faced after being in business for several years. Things were going pretty well. I had won a couple of trials and had a steady stream of business coming in from referrals. I was getting comfortable, but also complacent. I was not putting forth the same effort as on the day I started. In the beginning, I was so excited just to be in business for myself that even chores like shopping for office supplies at Staples were exhilarating.

I spent a lot of my time trying to cultivate new business by introducing myself to paralegals and accountants in the area. Within a few months, business started coming in and I was making respectable money, enough to satisfy most of my wants. However, as Tony puts it, you are either climbing or you are sliding. Although I was making enough money to do the things I wanted, I was missing the excitement the business originally gave me. Feeling myself sliding, I went back to basics and reviewed Tony's books and tapes.

Tiger Woods as a Role Model

The topic I needed to review again was Constant and Never Ending Improvement (CANI in Tony's acronym). I took Tiger Woods as my role model. He had faced similar issues after his great year on tour when he won over $6 million dollars and eight golf tournaments, including the PGA. Most people associated with the sport thought 1999 was an extraordinary year for Tiger, one that would probably not be duplicated. In fact, Tiger ended the year by winning three consecutive tournaments. I cut out a quote from Tiger in which he discussed his outlook for the 2000 golf season. In fact, I taped it on my computer screen so I could see it every day. What he said was: "My goal for 2000 is to get better and improve."

When I first read that quote, I could not believe he was serious. After all, he had just completed one of the best years in PGA tour history. To my mind, he should just be thinking about maintaining his level of excellence. But there is the crucial difference between Tiger and the rest of us. He is always looking for ways to improve. Although he may not know of Tony's work, he clearly embodies Tony's principle of CANI.

As everybody knows, Tiger had an even more amazing year in 2000. He won nine tournaments, three major championships, and extended his winning streak to six tournaments, including that great come-from-behind win at the *AT&T Pebble Beach Pro-Am*. Not to mention the nine million dollars he pocketed. When asked about 2001, Tiger said that he planned on improving in all categories: putting, driving, short game. He also said that he could not control whether someone else would have a great week, or whether he would get some bad breaks. His main goal is to improve his game and give himself a chance to win every week.

How many of us have this mindset each and every day? I certainly did not. Even with the modest success I had achieved and the improvements I made in various areas of my life, the principle of constant improvement was not embedded in my thinking. I had the attitude that many people have. I want to work hard for a while, hit some level of success, then relax and/or party. Fortunately, I had Tony's principles and Tiger to show me how to apply them. Since Tiger is one of my heroes (my BMW license plate frame says: "I AM TIGER WOODS"), it was extremely beneficial to hear what he had to say about self-improvement. I've noticed other fairly successful athletes who probably started partying too much after reaching a certain level of success. John Daly, for example, possesses skills similar to Tiger's. An extremely long hitter, with a great putting touch. If you play golf, you know this is an incredible combination.

But look what happened to John after he hit his pinnacle of success. Did you ever hear him talk about improving his game and getting to the next level? I never did. I only heard that he started drinking, eating and partying like it was going out of style. Did he try to improve his game? Maybe. But constant improvement did not seem to be the major focus of his life. Quite the opposite of Tiger. Fortunately, John has recently lost a lot of weight, stopped drinking and set himself on the road to recovery. I wish him the best of luck. I miss watching him play at his best. (John Daly has since won the *BMW Invitational* on the European Tour – Congratulations, John!)

We all need to have Tiger's mentality in our daily lives. The reason fans are so enthralled with Tiger is that he shows us what being outstanding looks like. We get excited watching him because we all know there is something we can be outstanding in. We just need to go out and do it every day. Consistently. Not just after declaring New Year's resolutions, or after hitting 40.

Think about where you would be if you had employed this kind of thinking since you were a kid. How many more skills would you have? Remember that Spanish or French class you took in high school? How much better would you feel about yourself now if you had taken it seriously and became bi-lingual? Would you be more marketable? I certainly would be making a lot more money if I had tried to be outstanding in the Spanish class I took, instead of just doing the minimum to get by. What about the piano lessons you took for a couple of months? Wouldn't it be great if you could play an instrument now?

What about your work skills? Do you try to get better at what you do each and every day? Or with your relationship at home? Or with your physical body? If you are not trying to improve yourself in all categories, then you are probably "sliding." That is where I found myself after being successful in business for several years.

The important thing is to take an honest look at yourself and ask whether you are making continuous improvement in each area of your life. This goes for everyone. Not just those who are beginning their success program, but even those of us who have employed Tony's techniques for the past ten years. Don't get caught in the "trap" of success. Even though you have accomplished many of your goals from last year or ten years ago, you still need to grow and improve. After reviewing Tony's lessons on CANI and hearing what Tiger planned to do in the year 2000, I began a new way of thinking. My primary goal for the new millennium was to make 2000 better than 1999. I planned to do this in all areas of my life. My business, my relationships, my finances, my physical body and my level of fun. I wanted to be able to say on New Years Day 2001 that I had made some definite improvements and accomplishments. I think that is the goal everyone should have each New Year. This is what I wrote in my success journal at the beginning of the year 2000:

BUSINESS

1) *Increase my income from the previous year by at least 20 percent.*
2) *Improve my litigation skills by doing several trials, reading books and attending at least one seminar.*
3) *Improve my productivity at the office by hiring an assistant to do the routine tasks at the office.*
4) *Increase my marketing efforts to one day per week.*

RELATIONSHIPS

1) *Take relationship with my girlfriend to the next level by getting engaged.*
2) *Continuously try to improve our communication and the fun activities we participate in.*
3) *Improve relationship with my parents and spend as much quality time with them as possible.*

4) *Increase the time I spend with my friends doing non-work related activities.*

PHYSICAL BODY

1) *Increase my running from 30 min./day, 2-3x/week to 40 min./day, 4-5x/week.*

2) *Cut down beef consumption to one dinner per week.*

3) *Stop eating before I am full.*

4) *Decrease coffee to one cup per day.*

5) *Increase water to eight glasses per day.*

FUN

1) *Try to have a least one day of the work week reserved for fun activities.*

2) *Plan something fun every day.*

3) *Reward myself for an outstanding week with something fun.*

These were some of the things I set out to improve upon. It was highly gratifying on December 31, 2000 to look back and see all the goals I had accomplished from my written list. By approaching the year with the same mindset that Tiger talked about, I had a clear outcome. The year 2000 was my best yet. Can you guess what my goal is for 2001? That's right. To have a better year than last year. I know it sounds simple. But you do need to make a conscious effort in order to improve. Not that there is anything wrong with being happy about your current situation. Tony says, "You should happily achieve, instead of achieve to be happy." But, the key to real success is the continuous improvement you make in yourself and your accomplishments. Just look at what Tiger did.

Perhaps the best way to connect with the proper way of thinking is to recall how you acted and felt your first day at a new job. I'll bet you were excited just to go to work, and you wanted to learn everything you could about the new job. You were determined to do well. I recently had a plumbing problem at my home and called a Roto-Rooter service. Two guys came over – one a seasoned professional and the other just starting his first day on the job. The new guy seemed so excited to be unclogging my drain. He was extremely polite, and I remember him taking the time to explain everything and inform me of other services his company had to offer. He listened to everything his trainer said and was obviously eager to learn.

Even with the most boring job in the world, on the first day I always felt a powerful desire to learn and improve. Unfortunately, it never lasted. Even with my own business, things started to get routine after a while.

Staying on the Top of Your Game

You need to have some type of success routine in place if you are going to be consistent and succeed long term. Although, it has been ten years since I began *Personal Power*, I still listen to that program at least once a year. There's a story about a guy whom Tony helped to stop smoking that illustrates this point. Tony spent thirty minutes one day with this chain smoker who then stopped smoking for over four years. When Tony ran into this fellow several years after their one and only consultation, the guy got right in his face and told him that his "stuff" doesn't work. After Tony got over the initial shock, he asked the man how long he stopped smoking, and the answer was: for about four and a half years. When a thirty-minute session gets a guy to stop for over four years, that is not failure. That is amazing success. The lesson here is that even after you start experiencing some initial success from *Personal Power*, you need to condition yourself regularly for a lifetime of success. Nowadays, whenever I begin to stagnate, Tony is always there, sitting in those nice little boxes, ready to come out and save the day.

Now I realize that I need to continually review the techniques in *Personal Power* and all the other personal development books I've read. This isn't something you can listen to once and make your life perfect. You need to keep reviewing the material even after you become successful. I'm not suggesting that you listen only to *Personal Power*. Tony would probably agree that there are many highly qualified individuals out there in the field of peak personal performance. You have to make this a ritual, something that you do on a regular basis. My personal success routine currently consists of the following:

1) I usually have a new book about success that I read for about 15 - 30 minutes per day. (See Chapter 16 for my recent favorites.)

2) I listen to one of Tony's CD's *(Personal Power, Unleash the Power Within, Lessons in Mastery, The Time of Your Life, Get the Edge)* while I am in the shower or in the car.

3) I listen to the goal-setting workshop in *Personal Power* every six months to refine my current goals based on the progress I have made.

4) I like to attend a "success oriented" seminar at least once per year, with Tony's being my favorite, of course. (see Chapter 21 on Robbins seminar).

5) I like to write in my success journal 4-5 times per week

and discuss my accomplishments during the week: what I failed to get done, my priorities for the upcoming week and all the magical moments I have experienced. (This helps to build up "success momentum.")

By keeping my mind occupied with the quality references contained in all the above materials, I am able to have a positive, motivated and energetic outlook every day. The key is consistency. Anyone can do this for a couple of weeks or maybe even a few months. However, if you can maintain some type of success routine for a couple of years, your accomplishments begin to multiply exponentially.

START YOUR SUCCESS ROUTINE TODAY!

One final note. It is April 8, 2001, and my man Tiger Woods just won the *The Masters* and completed a "Grand Slam" of all four professional major championships in golf (during the Tiger fiscal year).

When being interviewed after the tournament he was asked, "What was the key shot in your round?" To that he replied, "It was the drive on 13." (The shot was a power draw that soared around the dogleg.) Do you know why he liked that shot? Tiger said, "It's a shot I've been practicing the last couple of months, knowing the fact that I'm probably going to need that shot."

Who could ask for a more perfect role model for anyone striving for success. Tiger makes it look extremely cool to work hard and practice. Although I am not planning to compete on the PGA tour, watching Tiger and hearing about his work ethic, has motivated me to strive to be outstanding in my daily life. I know the one thing Tiger and I *can have in common* is to follow the same principle of constant and never ending improvement.

After accomplishing his great feat, people were asking him what it felt like to be the greatest golfer ever. Tiger replied that he didn't want to think he was the best ever at twenty-five since that didn't leave anything else to accomplish. Contrast this attitude to those other twenty-five-year-old athletes who think they are already the greatest in their respective sports.

Seeing Tiger win *The Masters* got me pumped like when I saw *Rocky*. (Do you remember people doing pushups in the aisles of the movie theaters?) But better, because it is real life. A non-fictional character who accomplished something that could go down in history as one the greatest feats in sports. I don't know about you, but I am going to keep improving myself like Tiger.

15

◆

KICKING BAD HABITS
&
CREATING GREAT ONES

We all know what we need to do. The problem is, sometimes it is hard to get yourself to actually do it. For instance, we know that we should work out, save money and not smoke, but it can be difficult to ditch bad habits and start good ones. I am sure most parents tell us that we shouldn't smoke (even if they do), and that saving money for a rainy day is a good thing. The problem is they rarely give us a step-by-step method for developing excellent habits.

Tony spends a lot of time in his *Personal Power* program discussing how we can change anything in our lives. His basic premise is that everything we do is related to avoiding pain and gaining pleasure. We overeat because it gives us pleasure. The only way we can control our food intake is to associate more pain than pleasure to overeating. Remember the last time you pushed your food away when you were still hungry. Why did you do that? Probably because you associated pleasure to limiting your food intake, and associated pain to pigging out.

You can use this technique to "repair" all of your bad habits. Simple as it sounds, it really works. However, the only way to make it work is to associate a lot of pain to your bad habits.

Feeling the Pain

Using Tony's method, it is essential to be extremely clear about all the pain you will experience or have experienced as a result of your bad behaviors. It's not enough to tell yourself that something is bad. You have to burn it into your brain. The technique I have used successfully is to write about all the pain in my success journal. When you write everything down it becomes more real. You can see all the things you are missing, or will miss out on in the future. Let me give you an example from my journal.

At one point I was struggling with myself about wasting money on unnecessary expenses – I had a bad habit of having food delivered all the time. For many people, this could be the equivalent of spending money on cigarettes. I wanted to eliminate this wasteful spending but found it difficult. I mean, it is so easy to spend an extra $4 per day because it doesn't seem like much. About the same as a pack of cigarettes. I spent an additional $30 per week because I was too lazy to pick up my own food. Initially, I would be able to eliminate the problem for weeks at a time. However, whenever the opportunity arose, this bad habit again reared its ugly head. What could I do? I referred back to Tony's program and took it very seriously. Rather than just think about it, I wrote down all the things I could have had in the past year, had I managed to control my spending.

By spending $30 per week on something I could have avoided, I lost the opportunity to:

1) buy a Big Screen T.V.
2) or a nice piece of Art
3) or a new computer
4) or a DVD player with 50 new DVD's
5) or 5 bottles of Chateau Lafite Rothschild
6) or 10 pairs of Kenneth Cole Shoes
7) or 5 dinners at Spago
8) or 10 bottles of Dom Perignon
9) or take a trip for 2 to Hawaii
10) or a cruise for 2 to Mexican Riviera
11) or see a Broadway musical every month
12) or see 15 movies per month
13) or attend 2 Tony Robbins weekend seminars

Wow, that is a lot of great stuff I could have experienced had I saved the $30 per week. What a waste of money that is when you look at it over the course of a year. (Of course, if you don't care for the items on my list, substitute what you would spend with about $1,500 and tell me if that is not painful to you.) It really hurt to look at that list. That was *pain*. All of a sudden there was no pleasure in wasting that $30 per week. Just like Tony says, it's all about pain and pleasure.

Establishing Good Habits

Curing bad habits is just one of the ways Tony enabled me to improve my life. By applying the same principles of pain and pleasure, I was also able to cultivate great habits.

Like many of you, I was a terrible student. I had the bad habit of waiting until the last minute to study for tests. I always tried to do the absolute minimum to get by in a particular class. (Just for your information, I had, back to back, 1.4 and 1.5 GPA's in college and almost got booted out. If it weren't for the "A's" I got in my Acting/Theater classes, I would have been in the "Square Root Club." You receive that dubious distinction when the square root of your GPA is actually higher than your GPA.)

I would have been kicked out of school had I not been subconsciously employing Tony's pain and pleasure principle. When I finally realized all the pain I would face (working at 7-11 and getting yelled at by my parents), I managed to get my act together and graduate as an average student.

Discovering Tony before I went to law school made things totally different the second time around. I went from being an average student to graduating cum laude with several awards for the highest grade in the class. Again, it all goes back to the pain and pleasure principles. Prior to Tony, I always thought of studying as a painful experience, one that I wanted to escape from as soon as possible so I could do other "fun" things. What I should have done was to associate fun/pleasure to studying. And that is what I did finally. Prior to my first semester of law school, I decided to write down all the pleasurable things that would result from studying. That's right, pleasure and studying in the same sentence.

———————◆———————

What pleasurable things will result from studying very hard and taking my education extremely seriously?

1) *You will be able to successfully complete law school (at first I just wanted to graduate since I barely made it through college).*

2) *You will be learning things that will directly result in your ability to have your own business.*

3) *You will have a second chance to show that you are better than the average student you were in high school and college.*

4) *You will be able to stop working in crappy jobs that you hate.*

5) *You will be in control of your own destiny if you can successfully complete three years of law school.*

I expanded on this list by writing down all the pain that would result if I did not study hard:

1) *You will have to go back to doing the job you hate.*

2) *You will blow a great opportunity to get the skills and knowledge you need to start your own business.*

3) *You will disappoint your parents again.*

4) *You will disappoint yourself again.*

5) *This may be your last chance.*

6) *You may never reach the goals you have set for your life.*

7) *You will have a hard time attracting and maintaining a relationship with a successful person because you are not at her level.*

8) *Your friends will all be doing much better than you.*

9) *You will be a loser!*

You can see the power of writing everything down. It is there for you to see. Plain as day. Remember how this enhances memory: if we hear something (e.g., if we say it to ourselves), we retain only 20 percent, but when we write it down our retention jumps to 70 or 80 percent. Now imagine how this exercise changed my thinking about studying. It was no longer something I wanted to avoid. I had clear reasons why it was a pleasurable thing to do, and why not studying would be painful.

Let me give you a typical study scenario that most students face during the course of a semester. Generally, you have a midterm and a final. The ideal student would try to review each day what he has learned in class and then do the assigned reading for the next day. The hard part is dedicating yourself to this every day, or nearly every day. The problem is, since there is no immediate deadline – the pain of an exam, most students put off their studies until a few days before the exam. Unfortunately, most people cannot perform at their optimum level on exams by studying at the last minute. (There are a few brainiac exceptions out there and you know who you are.) To do their best, most students need to slowly build this knowledge into their heads over the course of the semester. My problem was that I thought I was in the smarty-pants category. Because of some success in the past (studying at the last minute and doing well on an exam), I believed I could do this all the time, despite the many times the strategy backfired.

That was the first bad habit I needed to get rid of. Why take such a chance with my future? Why would anyone want to take the risk of not studying for an exam that will determine where he ultimately goes to college, or whether he will be able to become a lawyer or doctor? You can see my thinking now. I was beginning to associate considerable pleasure to studying and serious pain to not studying. This is what you need to do with everything in life: isolate the activities that need improvement and employ the pain/pleasure strategies to make the appropriate changes.

Think of where you could be today had you done that ten years ago. Or, where you could be in ten years if you start today. Luckily for me, I found Tony before it was too late.

16

◆

KEEP READING, KEEP GROWING

When I first began *Personal Power*, I remember Tony saying that he had read over 700 books in the area of personal development and psychology. At first, this was hard to believe. Didn't everyone say the same thing about success? How many different ways can you talk about goal-setting?

I have since retracted that belief. Tony makes it abundantly clear that if we are committed to success, we must study it. Granted, some books are forgettable. But many are excellent and have aided me greatly in designing my dream life. You'll be surprised how addicted you become to success-oriented material. Now whenever I go to the bookstore, I see several titles that interest me. The hard part is limiting myself to buying only one book at a time.

Although I believe in acquiring a variety of books, I do recommend that you focus on only one book at a time. The best way to finish a book is to make it a rule not to buy another one until you have done so. When you buy several books, it is so easy to read a few chapters of one and then move on to another, if the first one gets a little boring.

Of course the most important part of the reading process is applying the stuff you learn to your daily life. As Tony says, most people read a book, learn about many great ideas, and then never apply them. What a waste. You might as well have been reading a trashy novel. Use it or lose it! It is unlikely you will remember something you haven't put to use.

I have Tony to thank for making me a voracious reader on success, business, and psychology. I don't think I've read 700 books, but I've certainly read a lot. Without the lessons from *Personal Power*, I doubt I would have even embarked on such a learning journey. I remember when I started Tony's program, the last three books I read were *The Firm, The Pelican Brief*, and *A Time to Kill*. Great John Grisham books, but they were primarily for entertainment. Back then, I thought reading should only be for fun. I didn't think I needed to learn anything new. I figured that since I had already graduated from college, I'd already read everything I needed to, as far as learning was concerned. Boy, what a terrible belief that was. It is actually scary to think of where I might be today, had I not begun reading books geared toward success.

Back in 1992, when all of this got started, I wrote down the following in my success journal:

> *Must read at least 10 pages per day even if I am busy, tired, etc. I must do whatever it takes because I totally believe that if I continue to read, learn and improve every day, I have nowhere to go but to the top. You need to get momentum building and continue your success learning.*

Remember, whatever it takes. It's fun to learn. You don't want to be a loser, do you?

As I have said many times before, you really have to write all these things down in order to make your desire a reality. In the initial stages of my personal development, I read quite a bit more than ten pages per day. I really immersed myself into the whole success mentality. I still read quite a bit now, but much less than when I first began. Now, because of all the great opportunities I am fortunate to have, I spend most of my time actually applying what I learned in those books.

A Success Reading List

In order to get you excited about reading more books I want to tell you about some of the ideas that I have obtained from other authors. Thanks to Tony, I was able to discover these other gems of information which I have used to my great benefit.

Steven Covey –
The Seven Habits of Highly Effective People; First Things First

The best tip I got from Dr. Covey (and there were many) is one that I have shared with many people facing time management problems. In his book, *First Things First*, he discussed a lecture he gave his students. He had a fish tank in front of everyone and filled it to the top with some big rocks. He asked the class, "Can we put anymore stuff in?" The class said no. Dr. Covey then proceeded to put in a bunch of smaller rocks and pebbles. He asked again, "Can we put anymore stuff in?" This time they were a little smarter and said yes! The good doctor then put in a container of sand. He asked again, "Can we put anymore stuff in?" The class again said yes. Dr. Covey then emptied a container of water into the tank until it was filled to the top.

Now for the big question. Could you have put the big rocks into the tank if you'd started with the sand or the water? Of course not. Not without spilling the water out of the tank. What Dr. Covey wanted to illustrate was how important it is for us to "get the big rocks in first," i.e., when scheduling your week, write down the most important activities (the big rocks), those that will give you the greatest personal growth and happiness first, before adding in the less important (smaller rocks) into your schedule. Together with what I learned from Tony's *The Time of Your Life* program, this has been an incredible tool in speeding up the process to design my ideal life.

Harvey Mackay – *Swim with the Sharks Without Being Eaten Alive*

I got a great negotiation tip from Mr. Mackay that I used in acquiring my car (the now famous Mercedes SL convertible) and a piece of property. He writes about sending in a "clone," who will feel out the seller and obtain vital information that you can use when you go to make your purchase. For example, I sent my friend to a car dealer and had him make a low ball offer, one that would probably be rejected. It was, but the seller basically told him what his absolute bottom line was. This was of great benefit to me because I knew it was a fantastic price. I was able to go into that car dealer, confident of getting the price I wanted to pay. Why? Because I knew where to start the negotiations and when I could take a hard line on my price. Had I not sent in a "clone," I would not have been sure that my price would be accepted, and likely would have been talked into paying more. I might have spent $14 for that book, but I probably saved $2,000 on the car. Not a bad return on investment. That kind of information is not something you would naturally come up with yourself. I had never used that tactic in any negotiation I had been in before. Have you?

Tommy Newberry – *Success is Not an Accident*

Mr. Newberry has an excellent way of contrasting high achievers with underachievers. He states, "High achievers are motivated by pleasurable outcomes. Underachievers are motivated by pleasurable methods." How true! I realized that whenever I worked hard on something I was focusing on the *big goal*, e.g., passing the bar exam, finishing this book, or getting my body into amazing shape. Although there was some incredibly hard work involved, I managed to take action because of the pleasurable outcome I was visualizing.

However, in those moments that I am not proud of, I decided to take the easy route. Let's say I had a major project to complete at the office. When I chose to make it as painless as possible – for example, by working while talking to one of my friends or listening to sports radio I was at my least productive. During those times, I was motivated by pleasurable methods of reaching my goal. What I should have done was jump into my task completely by focusing on the pleasurable outcome (completing the big task that would eventually lead to some money). After reading Mr. Newberry's book, I was better able to consciously monitor my "motivation."

Here are a few of my favorite books from which I have derived extremely valuable information. I highly recommend them for your Success Library:

Napoleon Hill – *Think and Grow Rich*
Tom Hopkins – *The Official Guide to Success*
Richard Carlson – *Don't Sweat the Small Stuff; Don't
    Worry, Make Money*
Henriette Anne Klauser – *Write it Down, Make it Happen*
Steven K. Scott – *A Millionaire's Notebook*
Brian Tracy – *Maximum Achievement*
Jack Canfield, Mark Hansen, Les Hewitt –
    The Power of Focus
David Schwartz – *The Magic of Thinking Big*
Benjamin Franklin – *The Autobiography
    of Benjamin Franklin*
Jeffrey Mayer – *Success is a Journey*
Steve Chandler – *100 Ways to Motivate Yourself*
Thomas Stanley – *The Millionaire Mind*
Cherie Carter-Scott – *If Success is a Game,
    These Are the Rules*
Keith Harrell – *Attitude is Everything*

The one tip I like to give my friends who are just starting out is to read part of a motivational/personal development book every day. All it takes is ten to fifteen minutes each morning. The beauty of this is that you will be putting many great things into your head before you leave the house. Ever notice how when you start a day on the right note, everything goes great? It's all about momentum. If you are still a little lazy about pursuing your dream life, this is probably the easiest thing you can do. All you have to do is watch fifteen minutes less TV per day.

Many times when I have given this advice, a common response is, "I'm too busy with my job to waste time on extra stuff like that." Guess what, if you don't spend time with the right books, you'll probably stay exactly where you are right now. The same job, year after year. The only way to make *big changes* in your life is to first improve your thinking. Do you think Tony would be where is right now if he never started reading the first of those seven hundred books?

Any of the books I listed above would be great to have next to your bed for daily reading. I personally have read Tony's book, *Awaken the Giant Within*, so many times. When you know a book that well, you can go to specific chapters or sections when you think you need help in a particular area. For instance, when I felt that I wasn't sufficiently excited about my future, I would turn to the chapter entitled "Creating a Compelling Future." When I was feeling down about things, I would read, "Questions are the Answer," where Tony talks about changing our focus to what is great in our lives.

Reading Faster, Reading Better

Before we leave this chapter, let me pass on to you some of the best advice I ever received – helpful in every aspect of your life, whether or not you are still in school. *Take a speed reading class.* Sometime in early 1993, before I went to law school, I enrolled in an adult education speed reading class. On the first day, the instructor tested everyone on their current reading speeds. Mine was about 400 words per minute. Respectable, but not great. There was a high school student in the class who read at about 170 words per minute. We all admired his determination to be with a bunch of "old folks" in an effort to improve himself.

This was the best $59 I ever spent. By the end of the eight classes, my reading speed went from 400 to 1000 words per minute – and my comprehension stayed the same. (The high school student improved to about 700 words per minute – quadrupling his previous speed.) Next to Tony's teachings, speed reading probably helped me make the biggest improvement in my life. When I went to law school, I was able to complete the assignments in about half the time. Instead of studying for six hours a day, like some of my classmates, I was finished in three. Since I had to support myself at the same time, I really needed those additional hours to work my part-time job.

Just imagine how much better you would have done in high school if you could have read two, three or even four times faster. The kid in our speedreading class was probably able to finish his homework and still have plenty of time to have fun. Studying less and getting better grades. Why? Because if it takes you only two hours instead of four, you're probably going to be more focused during those two hours.

———◆———

Creating Time for Pursuing Your Goals

I bet many of you have given up on improving your skills because you don't have the time. Either your family or your job takes up too much of your day. What if you could study in one-third the time? Wouldn't that make it possible to go back to school?

I know it sounds too good to be true. We have all seen those Evelyn Wood speed reading classes on television. The ones that show students reading as fast as they can turn the pages. I'm here to tell you that it does work. It's just a matter of training your eyes to see more than one word at a time. My instructor told me that some people have increased their speed 10 times! I think the first obstacle she needed to overcome with her students was our belief that it couldn't be done. Once she proved to us that it was possible, everyone increased their speed. Even the worst student in the class doubled his speed after eight weeks. He probably didn't even practice between classes. I did not practice much and my speed went up 2.5 times. When you know you are a super-fast reader, your interest in reading increases tremendously. You know that you'll probably finish the next book you buy. Since I took that class, I've been able to read many more of the books that have helped me get to where I am today.

And don't stop there. There are many other low-cost high-quality adult education classes available in your area. The school I went to was called *The Learning Tree*. You're probably receiving their course catalogues in the mail. Look at them next time they arrive. There is an abundance of knowledge out there that is available to you at a minimal cost.

A friend of mine began taking art classes about eight months ago. Now he has an office full of paintings. Pretty good ones, too. Prior to taking the class, he never dreamed he could be "artistic." He may not make any money from it, but I know he derives a great deal of pleasure and relaxation from painting. He also likes to see people looking at them in amazement. My first reaction was, "You did this?"

The Thrill of Personal Growth

Nothing is more fulfilling than personal growth. I don't know what excites you. It may be writing, painting, acting, playing an instrument, or speaking a new language. Whatever it is – *take action!* Get started now so you can feel the pride of accomplishment next year, after you have mastered a new skill. Imagine yourself a year from now, having followed two different courses of action. One path is spending Monday nights at home watching TV. The other is spending two hours every Monday night learning to speak French.

Flash forward to a year from now. If you spent Monday nights watching TV, you probably can recall a few memorable shows, but nothing worth talking about. On the other hand, if you spent Monday nights learning to speak French, you have additional knowledge you could use to have an amazing trip to Paris. Most importantly, you will have something that no one can take away – a new skill that you are proud of. Even better, you will know that you can accomplish anything you set your mind to. Nothing will give you more confidence. French may not be your *tasse de thé* (cup of tea in French) but there must be some skill you are dying to learn. Next New Year's would you rather have watched all that TV or would you rather be able to paint?

Personal growth does not have to be something monumental to be satisfying. Just recently, I went to my dentist to get my teeth whitened for my wedding. I thought it would be great if I could look my best on the big day. It was a simple procedure. For a couple of weeks, I wore a bleaching tray in my mouth when I went to bed. It was barely noticeable. I followed that up with a one hour "Brite-Smile" treatment at the dentist's office. Wow! I went from having pretty decent teeth to having a smile like Julia Roberts'. In the grand scheme of things, this procedure did not require major effort or expense on my part, but it gave me immense pleasure and increased confidence.

One of my friends began the "whitening" program at the same time. It was a lot of fun to flash our teeth at each other as they began to improve. It helps to undertake a new skill or personal improvement plan with someone who can help monitor your progress. Although neither of us could really tell how white our own teeth were getting (because we kept looking in the mirror ten times per day) our buddy could observe and communicate the improvement. (We used Britney Spears as our role-model for the ultimate teeth.)

The same excitement can be generated by losing weight, learning a new skill, or getting a make-over. Whatever you do, make it fun – something you will want to continue doing and turn into a habit. The whole purpose of this book and Tony's work is for all of us to have a better quality of life. The easiest way to do that is to try to improve at the ground level in every area. Every little bit helps.

Let me end this chapter with something I learned from Shaquille O'Neal's book, *Shaq Talks Back*. In his autobiography, the "Shaq-daddy" mentions "living the dream life. The money. The fame. The fact that you're basically playing a kid's game for a living. But like every job, it can get old."

That was something I needed to hear. Although I believed I was living my dream life, running my own business and having time to do whatever I wanted, sometimes, as Shaq said, things got old. Things I used to dream about doing on a weekday, like going to the office at 11 a.m. or taking a Ferris Bueller's Day Off, no longer gave me the same charge. However, after hearing Shaq say that even his spectacular life could get old, I realized this was part of life and that I needed to do something about it.

In his book, Shaq talks about finding ways to motivate yourself for each challenge. He also says that Michael Jordan was the best at it. "Mike would take any little thing that someone said and create a challenge for himself. He kept his edge 'cause he just made stuff up in his mind." If it's good enough for Shaq and Michael, it's good enough for me. Yesterday Shaq finished a game where he was 13 for 13 from the free throw line. This is the same guy who set a record a few months ago for missing all 11 free throws he attempted in a game. Shaq decided he needed improvement and hired a personal coach to work on his free throw shooting. Hard work does pay off !

If I still haven't convinced you of the value of reading to improve your skills…would you listen to Leeza Gibbons?

I recently read an article in a Southwest Airlines monthly magazine that said Leeza reads two books per week. One is generally on personal development and the other is on parenting. In this article she was not talking about what she did before she became a celebrity. She was talking about what she is doing today, after becoming successful. Not only does she do this herself, but she says her whole family likes to read together before they go to bed. For those of you out there who have never considered reading personal development books for "pleasure," I hope this chapter has motivated you to start doing it on a regular basis. If someone like Leeza Gibbons can make time to read "self-improvement" books, don't you owe it to yourself to make some time to do the same?

17

◆

SHOOTING FOR SOMETHING EXCITING EVERY DAY

It is nice to know that through your hard work you have the ability to get the things you really want in life. If nice cars or houses don't motivate you, the same approach can be taken toward freeing up more time to spend with your children or being able to do volunteer work for organizations you believe in. The bottom line is that you need to figure out what will motivate you to take action on a daily basis.

For my wife, Katie, it is volunteering her time for the Make-A-Wish Foundation, an organization that grants the wishes of children with life-threatening illnesses. For example, one of Katie's best friends, Tiffany, was granted her wish to dance with Michael Jackson at his concert in 1986. Fortunately, she is one of the lucky kids who made it. I recall a day when my wife was not feeling well, and urged her to stay home and rest. But she insisted on going to the Make-A-Wish office. I remember being upset that she wasn't taking care of herself properly. When she had a full-time job she probably would have stayed home and taken the day off. I know I would have stayed home from work if I'd felt that bad. However, she was determined to do what she could to make the group's annual art auction a success. She had something super exciting to pursue. Despite being terribly fatigued, she managed to get out of bed and put in an outstanding effort for the Foundation. I figure there is something to be learned from her behavior.

Similarly, I have noticed that my best days have also come when I'm striving for something that excites me. Unfortunately, these days were not typical. Usually, they occur in spurts as a result of chasing something spectacular. As Tony says, we need to get ourselves into the proper state to perform at our best. The problem is that it is difficult to do this on a consistent basis without proper guidance. Yes, it is easy to get motivated when listening to one of Tony's seminars, but we don't always have Tony around whenever we need to get ourselves going.

The best way to get fired up is to have an exciting short-term goal – one that can be achieved in less than six months. As I discussed earlier, even people living dream lives like Shaq and Michael Jordan need to find something to get them motivated every day.

Let me give you some guidelines for this goal:

1) It had better be something that really gets your motor going,

2) Something that you keep thinking and obsessing about,

3) Something that you believe is attainable if you put in a lot of hard work,

4) Something that is in alignment with all your other lifetime goals.

In order to illustrate the power of this new approach, let me tell you about a super exciting short-term goal I attained. Like every red-blooded American male, I've always had the urge to buy the ultimate sports car. At the time, I was already doing fairly well and driving a nice BMW. However, one day that urge took over. I happened to be at a car dealer for some routine maintenance to my BMW. Since I didn't have a ride back to my office I decided to wait. Rather than read magazines, I took a walk around the lot and stumbled onto a beautiful white Mercedes SL500 convertible. Naturally, I had to sit inside and put the top down. It felt really good! I then went for an exhilarating test drive. I remember saying to myself, "Whatever it takes, I want this car."

As I was leaving the dealership, I realized that my dream car would cost me a lot of money. At the time, I did not have the financial resources I have now. And I was not about to hurt my budget and lifestyle just to pay for a nice car. Besides, my fiancée would not have allowed me to spend money that was budgeted for more important things – like a bigger home or our kids' college education fund – for a mere toy. And that was what it was going to be – a toy. I did not need another car. I had a perfectly fine BMW. When you really want something you'll do almost anything to get it.

And that's when my brain started working. What do I have to do in order to buy this car and still maintain quality of life we were enjoying? Let's see. If I spent a couple extra hours per week marketing my legal services, that could bring me more money in the future. In addition, if I made better use of the time I actually spent at the office (instead of wasting hours on the internet), I could generate enough additional billable hours.

That was the easy part, coming up with a plan to make the additional money. Anyone can get to this stage; the hard part is following through and getting yourself to take massive action. That is when the power of having something super exciting to shoot for kicks in. Something I knew was possible to achieve with some extra effort. The first thing I noticed was that I woke up excited to get started on my new plan. How often can you say you were excited to wake up and get to work? You really can be, if you're shooting for something you are obsessed about.

I know you may be asking thinking: I'm not in business for myself, how can I make additional money whenever I feel like it? As Tony says, it's all about pain and pleasure. The only reason you're not making more money is that you associate more pain to making money than to not making it. For instance, someone who is working a typical 9 to 5 office job could do the following:

1) Go to night school to increase your skills and earnings potential.
2) Get a second job nights or weekends.
3) Increase your effectiveness at current job to be worth more to your company.

Anyone can do these things, it's just that many choose not to.

Fueling Your Obsession

I found myself thinking about my goal all day long. This burning obsession can affect all your daily actions. What I noticed is that it made me more determined to get things done. I no longer wasted time on things that did not help me reach my goals. I can remember a Superbowl Sunday when I decided not to watch the game but instead to write a marketing newsletter, which I would use to solicit additional business. You don't miss the Superbowl unless you are really determined! And that was what was happening. At the office, I found myself working longer hours than normal. Although I could have gotten by with fewer hours, I wanted to do whatever I could to reach my goal as soon as possible. I didn't put things off the way I used to. All of sudden my time management became extraordinary. Whenever it seemed I was about to give up on something because it was getting late or because there was a Lakers game to watch, I thought about my beautiful sports car and kept on going. I remember going to all the dealerships in the neighborhood that offered my Mercedes convertible (I started calling it mine well before I actually got one). Not only did I test drive "my" car as much as possible, sometimes I went just to gaze through a window or sit in one of them. This really stoked the fire. The more I did this, the more excited I got. The excitement continued to build and, with it came an even more determined effort at work. It even motivated me to exercise harder because I kept telling myself (while I was running): More running – more energy – more productivity – more money – more Mercedes SL. Within weeks, I found that my productivity had increased and the additional revenue started to come in. Furthermore, I began taking on additional work that I might have passed on earlier. If I hadn't had a super-exciting goal, I probably would have been content to do only my normal amount of work. Immediately prior to falling in love with the Mercedes, I did as little as possible to get by.

My experience with the car exemplifies perfectly Tony's point about having specific goals and knowing why you want them. I knew exactly what I wanted and why. Simple. The reason this is such a great illustration is because it was something I was obsessed about. Had I not felt the urge to buy that "toy," I might have been content with the money I was earning at the time and not made any major effort toward increasing it. Different people get motivated by different things. I recall Tony talking about how he went from making $38,000 to $1 million in a year, simply because he and his wife had brought a new life into the world. He took extra initiative because he wanted his child to have all the things he had lacked. When I have my first child I will probably feel the same. Although I might be content with a certain amount of money for me, I am guessing that I will want to give my child every possible advantage.

It's important to have fun with your pursuit. As long as it makes you more productive and energetic, by all means shoot for an extravagant goal. Generally, people who have made major accomplishments are the ones who have extremely expensive tastes and needs. They know that the only way they can get what they want is to work night and day to accomplish their goals. There is nothing wrong with that. That is how this country was built. Remember what Gordon Gekko said in *Wall Street*: "Greed is good, greed is right, greed works…" Most people need to have something "greedy" to shoot for in order to get off their butts and take action.

Although Tony Robbins has accomplished wonders since the advent of *Personal Power*, he started out like you and me. Those of you familiar with his work will remember that famous train ride through Russia during which he wrote down all his goals on the back of a map – which he has shown participants at some of his seminars. I recall these goals included having a stretch limousine and living in a house with the sounds of crashing waves nearby. He had something super exciting to pursue and he really did take massive action to accomplish it.

Visualizing Your Goal Accomplished

I found that a great way to build momentum toward your goal is to start talking as though it will soon be in your possession. For instance, when I was working toward acquiring my dream car, I always said to my friends that I would let them borrow it for a big date or a "Ferris Bueller's Day Off." I would think about a particular event in the future and picture myself pulling up in my new car. I know this may sound silly (since I'm talking about a car), but this process can work with anything in your life. As long as you are super-excited and willing to work for it. Make it so real that you can actually taste it. The best way to tell if your goal really excites you is to see if it gets you out of bed, motivated to take action.

When I was working toward getting my car, I did not want to waste time on things that would not help me reach my goal, i.e., non-money making activities. I wanted "my" car as soon as possible. That is the type of desire you have to wake up with every day if you want success.

Although you may become obsessed with your goal, don't let your obsession get to the point where you will stray from your original well thought-out plan. By this I mean, if you have a plan to work hard and save a certain amount of money for a particular purchase, don't get impatient and decide just to finance the whole thing. The best part about having such a goal is not only getting it, but the amount of determination and hard work that goes into its attainment. Through this experience you will test your ability to translate an abstract goal into reality. You will be able to evaluate how you handle the obstacles that come your way. But most importantly, you will understand how the process works and know that the next time you set your mind to something you will have the know-how to accomplish whatever it may be.

I faced this temptation while pursuing my dream car. I had a plan to save a certain amount of money in order to make a comfortable purchase. The biggest problem I faced was that I got so excited about my goal I wanted it right away. Fortunately, I caught my breath and stuck with the original plan. Remember, if getting what you want, means mortgaging your future, it's certainly not worth it. Not only would it add unnecessary stress to your life, you would miss out on many of the valuable lessons a pursuit like this brings. After you have put in the hard work and make the necessary sacrifices, you will be confident about your readiness to take on the next challenge.

The energy and momentum I got from my car pursuit provided me with a couple of exceptionally productive months. Unfortunately, after I got the car, my motivation to make money took a nosedive. It was not until I realized I was no longer working toward something super exciting that I was able to get back in a productive mode. After the Mercedes, I got the travel bug and took a several extravagant trips. Right now, my major pursuit is to write the best book possible. I have been getting up every day extremely excited to get to my computer and write.

Isn't it interesting that all successful people talk about getting up early every day? That's not because they don't like sleeping. It's because they just can't wait to get started on their Big

Projects or Big Dreams. I used to be the king of sleeping. My typical schedule would get me up at 9 or 10 a.m. On weekends, I would sleep past noon. If you are not pursuing anything, why get up early? Only when you are obsessed about accomplishing something do you become one of those people who can't wait to get out of bed in the morning. I am not suggesting that you start by setting your alarm for 6 a.m. That's not how it works. You need to find that super-exciting pursuit first. Afterwards, waking up early will just happen automatically.

Some people reading this will say, "I already get up early every day. But I'm not making any money." It is not just about waking up early. You need to have the excitement of working on something you are obsessed about. Most people are just going through the motions. They struggle out of bed, go to work, do the minimum and come home. Naturally, you're not going to be thrilled to get out of bed with that kind of attitude. It's only when you can turn your job into an exciting pursuit that you will soon be maximizing your ability.

I'm sure you can remember a time in your life when you were operating at or near your full potential. Think about that time. You were probably in pursuit of something that excited you. Maybe it was a big promotion. Maybe it was an attempt to close a big sale. Maybe it was an attempt to start your own business. The problem with most people is that they are content with mediocrity. They don't put forth an outstanding effort because they are not going after anything beyond paying their bills. Before you start every morning ask yourself: What am I shooting for today? If you can't think of anything, you probably won't be motivated to work hard. Yes, you'll probably go to the office and do what you have to, but it's unlikely that you will attempt anything spectacular. The trick is to find something that turns you on – your "magnificent obsession" for that particular day. (And as far as the car is concerned, let me leave this chapter with a line from Ferris Bueller – "It is so choice, if you have the means, I highly recommend picking one up.")

18

◆

JUST DO IT

When I was a kid, writing a book was not one of my dreams. I didn't even enjoy writing. The prospect of writing a ten-page paper in high school terrified me. Even in college, I avoided classes that required a thesis or a big paper. So how did I come to write a full-length book?

It all starts with an idea. A subject that you have something to say about. As I mentioned earlier, this started as a thank you letter to Tony Robbins. But it kept getting longer and longer until I realized there was a book here. Of all I have accomplished this project required the most *Personal Power* to complete. That's because it was so easy to avoid working on it. I didn't need to do it for the money. I probably could have made more money if I spent the time on my law practice. However, like my love affair with the Mercedes convertible, it became an obsession.

So how did I manage to start and complete this book? Looking back over my success journal, I noticed that I wrote down the idea for it in March 2000:

3/3/00

> *Went for a thinking walk yesterday and came up with the idea and title for my book –* Thank You, Tony Robbins *– a personal memoir that the shows the value of following a success program/book. I think it will be a best-seller. My goal is to write it within the next three years and have it published. My book will discuss the success principles I learned from Tony & how I applied them. It will contain excerpts from my success journals.*

I wrote that 10 months before I actually started this book. Everything begins as an idea, which ultimately, through much planning and effort, gets translated into physical reality. The best part about reading something like this in your success journal is that it gives you incredible confidence to pursue another big goal seeing that you've done it before. I now feel I can accomplish whatever I write in my success journal.

Excited as I was about the title and the idea for this book, I didn't plan to start it immediately. In fact, I told myself that I would start writing it the next time I was in Paris, just for the extra motivation. You know, all the romance of writing à la Hemingway and Sartre, on the Boulevard St. Germain at Les Deux Magots – the writers' café.

Many people say they will start a major project after some significant date or event:

"I'll start working out when I turn 40."

"I'll begin dieting after the holidays."

"I'll write that book after I retire."

It's common to look for every possible excuse to push the start of a Big Project into the future. Few unsuccessful people take immediate action. The pain and pleasure principles I discussed earlier make the reasons clear.

Okay, so how did I go from having a great idea for a book (something that a lot people have) to sitting down and beginning to type? The answer was so simple that I can't believe it took me ten months to get started.

I had just begun listening to *Personal Power* for the umpteenth time. On the first day, Tony tells you to write down something you have been putting off and take a step toward its achievement. I was putting off the start of my book. Having been a believer for about nine years, I followed Tony's advice, and just did it.

No need to buy that super lightweight new notebook computer. No need to wait until all the planets were in the proper alignment. No need to wait until I was sitting at Les Deux Magots. One day in January 2001 I decided to take action while waiting for my car to be washed. I happened to have my computer in the car and simply started typing at the outdoor taco stand next door.

That was the best experience I ever had with Tony's program. It taught me that accomplishing something as big as writing a book can be so easy. Whatever your big project is, don't waste your energy preparing to start. Just begin immediately and use that momentum to keep going until you finish.

Do you remember in the movie *When Harry Met Sally...*, when Billy Crystal, on New Year's Eve, runs as fast as he can to find Meg Ryan. Upon finding her, he says, "When you realize that you want to spend the rest of your life with someone, you want the rest of your life to start as soon as possible."

The same thing goes for your Big Dream. When you know

exactly what you want in life, you need to start working toward it as soon as possible. Why wait?

This is the most important thing I want you to get from this book and from all of Tony's learning materials. When you have an idea or dream, make a start. Just do it! No matter how small that first step is. I wrote only a couple pages waiting for my car to be washed, and it turned into a book I'm proud of. Regardless of what anyone else thinks of it, I feel good about being able to set aside the time and take major action. Wouldn't you like to be able to say something like that?

We all have regrets about things we failed to follow through on. I wish I had learned to play the piano when I was a kid. My parents gave me the opportunity, yet I quit after six lessons. Now, I often think about how cool I could have been playing at parties, had I continued. I'm resolved not to let that happen anymore. When I want something, I am going to do everything I can to get it done. And I hope you do too.

Overcoming Daily Obstacles

I thought it might be helpful to discuss some of the challenges one faces in the midst of a major project such as a book:

Time

You will need enough time to accomplish a grand undertaking. I know you're probably saying, "I don't have enough time now even to see my kids. How can I write a book, learn to speak French, take acting classes?" First, let me refer you back to Chapter 13, where I discuss Tony's time management techniques. If you still can't find two to three hours for your Dream Project, *make the time*! No matter what your predicament in life, you can always make more time.

Despite running my own business, I was able to set aside about two hours a day two or three days a week for my Dream Project by deciding to wake up an hour earlier than normal. I changed my office hours to start and end an hour later. And presto! I got the two hours I needed. Since I desperately wanted to write this book, I skipped Lakers games that I normally used to watch in their entirety. I ate more lunches sitting at my desk. I missed a few of my favorite TV shows (or I taped them to save 20 minutes per hour by forwarding through the commercials). It can be done. I'm impatient now with people who say they don't have enough time. I have heard it so often:

"I'd really love to back to school, but just don't have the time."

"I've got a great idea for a screenplay, but I have a real job and don't have the time."

"I work 12 hours per day and don't have time to work out."

Prior to starting Tony's program I never paid attention to people making excuses. Since I used similar ones myself, I thought it was normal. In fact, I didn't think it was cool to sound too motivated. I'd always try to belittle those "gung ho, success-oriented" people by saying they were geeks or did not have a social life. How wrong I was! Now, it really disappoints me to hear someone making excuses regarding a lack of time. Especially when in relation to their Big Dream. I generally don't say anything unless someone wants my input. Even though I'm a big believer in everything that Tony and I write in our books, I think people have to take responsibility for their own lives. You can't cram personal development ideas down someone's throat. Better to simply lead by your example. Everyone will want to know how you "made it."

Coping With Negative Feedback

Many people will want to tell you how impossible your Big Project will be to accomplish. When I started writing this book, I kept it a secret for the first four months – partly because I planned to give it to my wife as a wedding present on our honeymoon cruise. Another factor was my desire to be totally positive and focused on my Big Dream. I had previously talked about writing a book in the future, but people aren't so negative when you talk about something you haven't started – probably because they don't feel threatened by it. You're just like them: you have a great idea but you're not acting on it. Naturally, I did tell several people after it was well underway, but by then my writing spirit could not be broken. Besides, I needed someone to edit the book. You can't rely only on Spell check!

Staying Motivated to The Finish

Staying motivated was never a problem for me. Once I started, I kept writing like a man possessed. There were many times when I wanted to write but couldn't due to my trial schedule or because I was trying to keep this book a secret. I'm convinced that when you know what you want and why you want it, nothing can stop you. To make my resolve even stronger, I wrote in my success journal why this would be an amazing book:

1) *This will be the most amazing wedding present in the history of matrimony because it will show my girl that I can accomplish a major project.*
2) *Whether or not this book is a best-seller, I will prove to myself that I am a man of action and can accomplish what I set out to do.*
3) *I believe this book can help many of Tony's students when they see exactly how* Personal Power *helped someone like themselves go from rock bottom to achieving his dream life.*
4) *I believe this book will do extremely well because it has a great title and deals with a subject that will grab the interest of many people.*

The closer you get to your goal, the more real your vision of it will become. That's when the serious excitement begins. Tony talks about success momentum and how one success stacks up on another. This is what I started to feel. It is a beautiful feeling. One that I hope you will be able to experience with your endeavors.

Now you may think that a major project like writing a book or having your own business is something you will never be able to do. You may think it is only for extraordinary people, those who were born with some God-given talent. But I was a C student in English/Writing. I was totally lost, with no direction. Worst of all, I visualized my future as mediocre at best. All of that turned around. Tony had a big part in that.

But Tony's wisdom alone is not enough. You need to make the decision to take action. I could have listened to Tony until I was blue in the face, but if I never started to take action, I wouldn't be writing this today. Your Big Dream can happen too, Just do it!

Empowering Yourself to Dream Big

Not yet sure you can accomplish your big dream? Let me review an exercise I learned from Tony's *The Time of Your Life* program. I believe it will give you the certainty – and thus the confidence – to make your Big Dream a reality. In it, Tony instructs you to write down a list of things currently in your life that at one time were just dreams, desires or goals.

Here is what I jotted down prior to writing this book that gave me the confidence and certainty that I could accomplish such a major task:

Write down all the things which were at one time just dreams:
1) *To have my own business.*
2) *Becoming a lawyer.*
3) *To be making enough money so that I can do what I want when I want.*
4) *To travel as much as I want.*
5) *To be in total control of my own destiny.*

6) *To have a super exciting, fulfilling relationship with a beautiful lady.*

7) *To wake up before 6 a.m. and run 3 miles.*

8) *To own real estate.*

9) *To have money in my savings account for a rainy day.*

10) *To drive a Mercedes convertible and a BMW.*

11) *To take the LSAT and be accepted into law school.*

12) *To graduate from law school cum laude.*

13) *To pass two bar exams (CA, NV) on the first try.*

Prior to beginning Tony's *Personal Power* program, all of these things were just dreams and desires. I couldn't even call them goals because they seemed so far out of reach at the time. When I first started listening to Tony, I didn't think there was a chance in hell I would become a trial lawyer, with my own business and the time and money to travel on thirty-six vacations in five years. I didn't think I would ever own real estate. (You remember that I actually got turned town for a car salesman job because of my bad credit!) Nor did I think I would be driving a Mercedes SL 500 convertible *and* a BMW. I was struggling to pay for my 1983 Volkswagon. At the time, I was barely surviving on $1,000 per month, with no idea of what I was going to do in the future.

Doing this exercise provided the certainty I needed to write this book. No matter where you are in your own life right now, I urge you to do this exercise, right now. You will be amazed what it will do for your confidence.

◆

◆ Write Down All The Things Which Were
at One Time Just Dreams ◆

Hey, we're not done yet! Tony's next instruction was to take two of the items I thought were virtually impossible and write down the steps I took to make each one a reality. Here's one example I used:

Becoming a lawyer
1) *Deciding I wanted to do it, with the help and advice from my parents.*
2) *Studying for the LSAT every day for four weeks.*
3) *Working hard on my law school applications.*
4) *Working part-time to pay for living expenses.*
5) *Studying hard to get good grades – graduating cum laude.*
6) *Studying like crazy – up to 14 hours per day – to pass 2 bar exams on first try.*
7) *Completing all requirements to get licenses.*

• Your Two Major Dreams That You Have Achieved •

1)

2)

• The Steps You Took to Achieve Each Goal •

1)

2)

The purpose of this exercise is to show you that you have the ability and the know-how to accomplish your Big Goals. You have probably already done so in the past. There is no reason you can't do it again. As Tony says, "You have learned a system for managing your life to get the ultimate results you are committed to."

After I finished this exercise, I realized that I have been successful in the past in accomplishing what seemed, at the time, virtually impossible goals. When I started this book, it really seemed to be an impossible goal. But throughout the process I have been confident that I could complete this major task simply by remembering all the "impossible" things I previously managed to achieve. By following this system and simply applying what you have learned in accomplishing your prior goals, you, too, can achieve the "impossible."

19

◆

THE POWER OF
VISUALIZATION

Sometime in late 1999, I decided to propose to my girlfriend, Katie. I wanted to make my proposal something she would remember fondly forever. Something she would be excited to tell all her friends and family about. But most importantly, I wanted it to be the best surprise of her life. Being a big *Love Boat* fan, I decided to make my proposal on a cruise.

That's when my visualization process began. Initially, I pictured being on the cruise and proposing on the deck, hearing the waves crashing, with the stars overhead (a pretty familiar scene from *The Love Boat*). The next step was arranging the cruise well in advance so that she would not think it was anything other than a regular vacation. I brought up the idea about six months prior to the big day. Now that I had set the stage, I needed to fill in the details. What about the ring? That was difficult. I wanted to get something she liked but without having to be too inquisitive, since I wanted it to remain a surprise.

This is when knowing exactly what you want, well ahead of time, really pays off. During the next couple of months, at opportune moments, I made a few inquiries. They were subtle, but I did find out exactly what she wanted. Had I not planned well in advanced and known my outcome, it would have been extremely difficult to pull off the big surprise. During these months, my vision of how I wanted to propose became clearer and clearer. The words I would say that night slowly came to my mind, until I knew exactly the ones. I even knew what clothes I would be wearing. The details were coming into focus. I probably visualized this scenario at least once a day for several months.

As the big day drew closer, it was time to buy the tickets. When I spoke to my travel agent, she showed me the various rooms available through Holland America.

(By the way, the crew on our ship, the *M.S. Zandaam,* were great. When a couple gets engaged on their ship they become instant celebrities – we were invited to several exclusive parties thrown by the Captain.)

Looking at the brochure, I saw exactly what I wanted. The perfect accommodations for the big night. Although it cost about 50 percent more money, I opted for one of the biggest suites the ship had to offer. It was amazing: marble floors, spacious living area, a Jacuzzi. And most importantly, an enormous verandah, where I would pop the question. Now my vision was becoming even more exciting. I pictured our engagement taking place on that spacious verandah. As I read the cruise brochure, I noticed that they had a formal dinner, followed by a Broadway-style show planned for the first night. I decided to go for it on the first night for two reasons: 1) it was my mom's birthday (June 3), and 2) I just couldn't wait any longer, having pictured and reviewed this moment in my head for many months.

The agenda that preceded the big event was in focus. Add to that the champagne chilling in the room, and it was getting better and better. The only thing missing from my vision was the ring.

I knew I had planned the perfect evening, so I needed to get the perfect ring. Being a typical guy, I really didn't know what was exciting as far as rings were concerned. Fortunately, I had time to learn. I began doing a lot of shopping. Of course, the first place I looked was at CostCo. Their rings seemed like really good deals, but I didn't think they would match the intensity of the evening. I started looking around the shopping malls but could not find anything that excited me. Fortunately, a couple of random events pointed me in the right direction. I saw the movie *Sleepless in Seattle* (which, by the way, was written by a Tony Robbins student, Jeff Arch, immediately after attending the *Date with Destiny* seminar). In it, I saw Bill Pullman get Meg Ryan a ring from Tiffany's. Shortly thereafter, one of my friends was talking about how she buys all her jewelry at Tiffany's and wished she had gotten her diamond ring there. So off to Tiffany & Co. I went.

At first, I was a little scared even to walk inside the store since everything looked so impressive. But I gathered the courage and started to browse. I tried to avoid eye contact with the salespeople because I didn't want to be noticed. Even though I like to think of myself as a guy's guy, I was excited about seeing what they had to offer. Since I was able to ask my fiancée several key questions during the preceding months, I knew she wanted a square-ish diamond in a platinum setting. Luckily for me, Tiffany's had just come out with their latest design, "The Lucida," which looked exactly like the description Katie gave me. When the saleslady took it out of the display case, I knew this ring matched the intensity of the evening I had already laid out. It was a bit of a stretch, but I know my Katie was worth it!

Now I could visualize the entire evening, down to the last detail. It was soon to become a reality. I am happy to report that the evening went exactly as planned (though she did remark later that I seemed a little nervous).

After a magnificent dinner and Broadway-style show, we went back to room. I opened the bottle of champagne and we proceeded out onto the verandah. With the stars shining above and the waves crashing, I got down on one knee and popped the question. And fortunately (after seven months of planning) she said yes. I will leave the really juicy details to your imagination.

I hope that my engagement story has illustrated the power of visualization. It is highly unlikely the evening could have been such a memorable success had I gone about it haphazardly. Not only do you need to know exactly what you want, you need to visualize it many times along the way so that you can fill in all the magnificent details. I have since used this technique when working toward all my big goals.

Prior to the completion of this book, I constantly pictured my book being sold on Amazon.com and Barnes and Noble.com. I visualized it being reviewed favorably by the *New York Times* and saw myself appearing on *Oprah* as a guest after she included my book on her recommended list. Whether these things really happen or not is unimportant. The key is to get a clear picture in your mind, one that you can review over and over again, which will improve your vision and give you the best chance of accomplishing your Big Dream.

20

$\blacklozenge$

DEVELOPING SUPERMAN ENERGY

One of the greatest moments in sports history is the final shot taken by Michael Jordan. I'm sure you have seen it many times in the Gatorade commercial, where they ask, "Do you have what it takes to finish?" Did you also notice that Michael seemed to get better as the game progressed? When everyone else was beginning to tire in the fourth quarter, he was able to get to the next level and take control.

He wasn't necessarily born with all this energy. He continually worked on increasing it. Even when he was a mega superstar, he still pushed others to join him early in the morning to train. Why? Because he knew that to be the best you need to have more energy than everyone else.

We should always be looking for that edge over the competition in every aspect of our lives. Thanks to Tony's influence, increasing my energy has improved the quality of my life in both work and play. In *Personal Power,* he devotes a whole day toward increasing your energy.

Prior to beginning Tony's program, I did no aerobic training. The last time I ran was in high school, since it was required to pass the Phys Ed course. I was in decent shape. Every now and then I would get the urge to lift weights, but only managed to keep it up for two or three months at a time. I did play golf occasionally, though I rode in the cart most of the time. Not what you would call an energetic lifestyle. The sad part was that I really didn't know how little energy I had and what my potential was.

Once I started listening to *Personal Power,* Tony did a great job convincing me of the need to start exercising. You remember his story: he was thirty-eight pounds overweight and had little energy. But then he took that magical run on the beach and started to develop the energy we see now.

Building Up Slowly

I started my own energy program slowly. It is highly recommended that anyone who decides to begin a program like this consult a doctor first. (Since I am a lawyer, I'm especially conscious of the need to include a warning like this!) My goal for the first couple of months was to jog slowly for ten to fifteen minutes (about one mile). Within a few days, I began to feel my energy increasing. I slowly increased the speed and length of my runs, usually by only a block or two each time. Since then, I have been able to run for over an hour and for distances greater than 10 miles, and I'm fairly confident that I could run farther if I wanted to.

———————◆———————

Currently, my routine is to run about three miles (30 minutes), four to five times per week. The benefits have been tremendous. I have the energy to work as hard as I need to. More importantly, I have energy to do whatever fun things I can plan each night. If you are going to learn only one thing from Tony (or from me), it should be the value of increasing your energy.

The trick is to make your program as painless as possible in the beginning. Tony talks about someone whose initial goal was to run to the first light post on his street. Now the guy runs marathons. Another great example I have seen firsthand is my father-in-law. Although he is over 60 and retired, he can still outrun a young pup like myself – when he wants to. (He also can kick my butt in golf.) Like many Americans, he was a typical, slightly overweight man with a cholesterol problem. He didn't begin working out until his doctor told him, "You'd better start exercising and eating right, or you won't be around much longer." As Tony would put it, that created the pain necessary to make exercising a must.

My father-in-law started slowly. It took him an entire month just to build up to running one mile. But guess what? Within a year, he ran and completed a twenty-six-mile marathon. And that's not the best part. The guy is always happy and full of energy. It's hard to be an unhappy person when you have so much energy to spare. You should see him with his grandchildren. Because he started running, he will actually be able to enjoy them for many years to come. Better yet, with all this energy, his retirement is one long vacation. He plays golf almost every day during the summer. He takes his grandchildren to the zoo, to the amusement park, to baseball and hockey games. He baby sits. And still manages to run four miles five times per week. How many people out there are under 35 and can't imagine doing all that?

Breathing to Build Energy

Another energy-building technique I learned from Tony is deep breathing. At first, I was like most of you – distinctly skeptical. How could deep breathing increase my energy? I thought it might help me relax, but I doubted it would really affect whether I could go that extra mile. Luckily for me, by that point I trusted Tony.

His breathing technique is simple. You take a deep breath, hold it as long as you can, and exhale slowly. Tony recommends the following ratio: Inhale for 1x, hold for 4x, and exhale for 2x. I generally inhale for five seconds, hold for twenty, and exhale in ten. You may need to work up to this level. And it's so easy to do. I practiced it while I driving to and from work. Approximately fifteen deep breaths, two or three times per day. I started noticing the benefits within just a couple of days. At the end of each day I had extra energy. Where I normally tired, now I didn't. It's a great feeling to be at work at 7 p.m. and still feel you could keep going – if you wanted to.

Whenever I hear a friend complain about being tired, I always tell him or her about this technique. It's easy and doesn't take much time. In fact, it gives you something to focus on in traffic, instead of the traffic itself. Tony does a good job explaining the benefits of increasing oxygen to your blood cells. But I like to think of it in simpler terms. Did you ever see NFL players on the sidelines using oxygen when they get off the field? This works on the same principle. Anything that increases the oxygen in your bloodstream is good. Try it and find out for yourself.

———————◆———————

Drinking More Water

Another great thing you can do for yourself is to increase the amount of water you drink every day. This is another of Tony's big preoccupations. No need to bore you with the scientific details about the importance of drinking a lot of water. Tony tells you about all that in *Personal Power.* Oprah Winfrey includes an entire chapter in her book *Making the Connection,* just about drinking water. All the physical fitness books recommend the same thing. Because our bodies are comprised of about 70 percent water, we require about eight glasses of water a day to stay in optimal condition. The problem is that most of us find it rather difficult to drink that much water. I personally drank about one glass a day before *Personal Power.* Now, I squeeze in six to eight glasses per day, on average. The trick is to make it a priority during the day. That means consciously focusing on it. I went even so far as to list drinking eight to ten glasses of water every day as a major goal in my success journal. Start slow, but by all means get to at least six glasses per day. You will feel the difference immediately.

(If you are interested in improving your energy and physical body, I highly recommend that you attend Tony's living health seminar. It is packed with a lot of information from a number of top health and fitness experts – synthesized by Tony.)

Benefits of an Energy Bonus

If getting your body in great shape and living longer is not motivation enough, consider all the other benefits that increasing your energy will bring to your life. Increased energy can make a dramatic improvement in the quality of your work, and thus your potential earnings. Remember, it does not take a lot to differentiate an average worker from a great one. If you could have that edge of additional energy, you might be able to take the extra initiative to get the job done right.

I noticed in my law practice that having extra energy has increased my income dramatically. Prior to building my energy to its current level, I found it easy to call it a day when I began to tire especially since I have my own business. However, with increased endurance, what used to be difficult has become much easier. I have enough energy to complete my work and still turn on the after-burners to look for more business.

Of course this new-found energy can also increase your enjoyment of life. You may know some people, maybe even yourself, who go through life with little entertainment, simply because they can't muster the energy to go out and have fun. The typical 9-to-5 worker comes home, has dinner, watches television and goes to bed, only to start the same cycle the next day. For these folks the mere thought of going out and meeting people or engaging in other forms of recreation is exhausting.

Once you begin your energy buildup, be sure to continue increasing your endurance. Don't think you're Superman just because you can jog a few miles. I learned this the hard way. Although I managed to get myself into pretty good shape, I discovered that I needed even more energy several years ago while I was in New York City. At that time, I was a single guy and wanted to be known as Mr. Party and Mr. Electricity. A group of us were in a nightclub and I noticed one of my friends, Mark, dancing up a storm. It was 5 a.m.! I was slouched in a chair watching him with amazement. Why was he still full of energy? Had he listened to Tony Robbins? Even though I thought I was in good shape, being unable to keep up made me feel like a party pooper. I later found out that Mark spent a lot of time on aerobics since he taught jazz dancing on the side. That night I decided I was going to be the man with all the energy at 5 a.m. Since then I have taken great steps toward never running out of gas. When I got back from New York I made a conscious effort to increase the intensity and distance of my workouts, and this has taken me to another level. I'm not suggesting that everyone needs to party till 5 a.m. I don't do that very often myself anymore. But the key is to have the option.

I decided that staying in top physical shape was not only a priority for today, but one I should focus on for a lifetime. My Aunt Cleo has been a great role model for me in this. She has been working out for the past thirty years approximately five times a week. Now that is consistency! Despite the fact that she is close to my parents' age, she can still run circles around most people. I don't think I have ever seen her tired. We recently went hiking in the Santa Monica mountains. It was an hour's hike to get to the top and another hour to get down. There were some extremely steep areas and I saw many younger people quitting half-way up. When we finished she wasn't even breathing hard. In fact, she played tennis later that day. That's the type of energy I want to have twenty-five years from now. Find your role model!

Another useful tip. I actually came up with this one myself: Never, and I mean never, say you are tired. By eliminating the word from your vocabulary, you will always feel that you can persist in whatever you are doing. (Again, be sure to check with your doctor before you do anything beyond your current, normal activities.)

When you say that you are tired, or even say you think you are getting tired to someone, it becomes a self-fulfilling prophecy. You actually start to feel fatigued. I'm not suggesting that you will feel full of energy at 1 a.m. just by not admitting you are tired, but it will help. When you combine this mental attitude with the other points I have discussed – e.g., aerobic conditioning and deep breathing, you will literally become unstoppable. Better yet, you will have much more fun because you will have the energy to do things you enjoy.

Let me give you a great example of when this has worked in my life to perfection. My fiancée and I went to Europe in the Spring of 1999. Before the trip, I told her we had only one rule. We will not utter the words, "I am tired," for the entire trip. Our plan was to have the time of our lives, seeing and doing as much as was humanly possible during those two weeks. It worked. We were literally energizer bunnies for the entire vacation. Although we drank a bottle of wine every night with dinner, we still had enough gas in the tank to stay out late and wake up early the next day. For those of you who know Paris pretty well, we actually toured Versailles and the Louvre on the same day!! That was our most impressive display of energy and endurance.

It's helpful to have some special event in the future to work out for. This will help motivate you to stick with your program. My own best months of working out were when I had specific events to get myself in shape for – for example, my wedding.

One last tip: the best way to kill your energy is to overindulge in a big meal. You need to plan your eating habits not only for the proper weight management but, more importantly, to maintain maximum energy throughout the day. After a big lunch the last thing you want to do is get back to work. That happens when we don't consciously plan how much we are going to eat.

I developed this awareness while I was studying for the bar exam. If you haven't heard, this is a grueling eighteen-hour exam spread over three days. It was not unusual for me to be studying twelve to fourteen hours per day during the few weeks that preceded the exam. Here's where proper eating really makes a difference. During one of my hardcore study days, I had just completed five straight hours in the morning and was prepared to have lunch. One of my friends said she would take me out for a great sushi lunch as her way of wishing me luck. Now I love sushi and I ate like there was no tomorrow. When I returned to my office to study, the only thing I wanted to do was lie on the couch and put my feet up. Despite my super-motivated and productive morning, I wasted the whole afternoon feeling lethargic.

Normally this would be no big deal and I would chalk it up as a lazy day. But now the stakes were extremely high. I couldn't afford to waste four prime time hours of studying. It could end up hurting my whole future. That's when I made the decision that I would no longer allow myself to be undisciplined with my eating habits. For the last few weeks before the exam, I methodically planned all my meals. A banana and orange juice in the morning. A small sandwich and pretzels (not potato chips) for lunch. And a few sushi rolls for dinner. The amount of each meal was controlled so that I would still be a little hungry at the end. Most importantly, my eating did not affect the momentum of my studying. I was just as motivated after eating as before. I believe that controlling my diet to study effectively was an important factor in my passing the bar exam on my first try.

My dietary limitation had nothing to do with trying to shed

some pounds. I'm actually a slender fellow who can eat as much as I want without gaining weight. (My fiancée doesn't like to hear that!) This is all about eating the right quantities to maintain a consistent level of energy throughout the day. I'm not saying that you need to be this rigid every single day. It's okay to pig out once in a while. But when you need to maintain peak performance throughout the day, you'll want to keep your intake to a minimum.

Begin your Superman energy program
today and see how amazing you can be!

21

◆

SEEING TONY LIVE

The most exciting events I recently experienced have been: the 2000 Democratic Convention, a Lakers Playoff Game and a Tony Robbins live seminar. And I must admit, for the number of people present, Tony's seminar was by far the loudest and most intense. I had no idea what to expect when I went to my first Tony Robbins event. Having read his books and listened to his CD's, I figured that it would be educational and interesting, but what I experienced blew me away.

The first seminar I attended was *Competitive Edge,* which is geared primarily for salespeople. It dealt with the power of influence on yourself and others.

Tony came on stage to an incredible roar. Louder than any rock concert I have been to with a comparable audience. Before discussing the sales material for the day, he talked about things I'd heard previously on *Personal Power* and his other CD's. But as Tony often says, "Repetition is the mother of skill," so it was good to hear it directly from the horse's mouth.

The most impressive part about the seminar was the amount of energy this man has. I figured he could maintain this rate of intensity for a couple hours, get us pumped up, and then settle into a more relaxed state. It never happened. We started at about 8:45 a.m. and, with only a one-hour lunch, we ended after 8:00 p.m. Hard to believe he could keep going at that pace for almost twelve hours. I was getting a bit tired just listening! Not only was he doing his thing on stage, but whenever he really wanted to pump up the crowd, he would run up and down the aisles at full speed, giving everyone high fives.

His ability to sustain this energy level for twelve hours was the highlight of that first seminar. After seeing that display, I understood how Tony could accomplish so much. I also thought, How could anyone *not* be successful with all that energy? I kept thinking if I could do my work every day, with such vigor, I would be making three times more money. I used to believe I had plenty of energy, but seeing Tony live, gave me a glimpse of the potential we all have.

Although this was a "sales" seminar that lasted close to twelve hours, I noticed that everyone, including myself, was attentive and alert for the entire day. I was surprised to be so awake after such a long day of "class." Normally, when I attend a class such as this, I'm dying to get to each and every break. And I usually try to sneak out before the end. Not this time.

Tony's teaching techniques were different from anything I had experienced. He really does keep his students "spellbound," as Kenneth Blanchard *(One Minute Manager)* has said. He begins the day by making sure you are wide awake and acquainted with all your neighbors. How does he do this? First of all, he cranks music that the Lakers Girls normally dance to. Then he asks everyone to give their neighbor a hug or a high five. There were no mere handshakes at this event.

Finally, he gets everyone to jump up and down like maniacs to his favorite party tunes. (By the way, Tony does have good taste in dance music.) We certainly got our blood flowing. It literally felt like a big party. Everyone, even the most conservative people, emerged from their shells, and went all out.

It wasn't all fun and games, of course. Tony discussed serious and helpful sales-related material throughout the day. His content was well organized and presented in our handouts in outline form. I learned some techniques that I have applied in getting new business for my firm. During the seminar, Tony instructed us to get into groups and try to sell our neighbors on whatever it was we sold. I was one of the few trying to sell legal services. Most people were selling real estate, office equipment or advertising. For most of us it was a great learning experience.

I noticed that most of the attendees had an overwhelming desire to improve themselves. These people really wanted to be at the seminar. I went there thinking I was the only one who totally believed in what Tony was teaching. I was wrong. Before I saw and heard all those screaming fans, I did not realize what a phenomenon Tony is.

Besides witnessing Tony's amazing energy, the next most important thing I learned and experienced first hand was the importance of getting into "the right state." Although I'd heard a lot about state management in *Personal Power,* I really didn't see how powerful it was until that seminar. What Tony tried to explain was that we need to be in a peak state to perform at our best in everything, including learning. Here, Tony cranked up the music and got us into a peak state about every 45 minutes. It seemed that whenever we might have been losing our energy, he got us right back into optimum state. Imagine if we could have someone to monitor and amplify our state management every day. How much more would we be able to accomplish!

Following the seminar I was so pumped up, I called my friend Dante from my car and our conversation (mostly of my excitement) motivated him to sign up to see Tony in Chicago with me. Here's what I wrote in my success journal immediately following the seminar:

Went to see Tony Robbins live for the first time at the Universal Amphitheater. It was an amazing experience. In addition to teaching us some great sales techniques, he displayed energy and enthusiasm for over eleven hours. Wow! I certainly got my money's worth. The most important thing I learned again from Tony is that you really need to be in a peak state to do your best! I recall that I was in a peak state for my GG closing argument and that's why I kicked butt!

I must be able into get in a peak state every day so I can be at my most productive. You should never do something in a stupid state. Why would you want to? I feel super energized and calm, while at the same time I know that I am on my way to success on the grandest scale. Remember, there is no success unless you can be grateful for whatever you have right now and along the way. Another thing I learned is that you can go all out for eleven hours and not be tired. Tony showed us that he has incredible energy to accomplish his goal of giving us an amazing learning experience. The key was to be sure that we were in a peak state most of the day via loud music/dancing to get pumped up.

I have my own office – I should be able to crank it up several times per day to work at a peak state for over 10 hours – if I want to. My goal for the week is to get in a peak state at work and try to maintain it all day to see how much more can be accomplished. Why would I want to operate at anything less than my peak state? First of all, you love what you are doing (unlike some lawyers/slaves who work for big firms and complain all the time about working too much). Second, it's your business – something that you have dreamed about having for over a decade. I make the decisions. No one tells me what to do – that rocks! Remember the key is to have the time and money to do everything you desire in your life.

By focusing on staying in a peak state all day, you will get to your outcomes much faster. Instead of taking 5-7 years, it could take as little as 2-3 years. Why would you want it to take longer? I feel great about taking the initiative and making the investment to spend a full day learning tools and ideas that can take me to the next level! As long as I have this constant and never ending improvement attitude, there is no freakin' way I will not succeed. And I'm talking about succeeding Big Time!

———————◆———————

Sustaining The High

Boy, was I motivated the next couple of weeks. The extra money I made from that injection of enthusiasm more than paid for Tony's seminar. Let me be the first to tell you that this was not just about hype and "positive thinking." Tony abhors (and even makes fun of) people who are just positive thinkers. It is especially ridiculous when you see these people so positive when they really have nothing to be positive about. On the contrary, Tony gives you something real to be positive about. By starting with your physical body and asking the right questions, he gives us the proper physiology and psychology to really be positive. Contrast this with your typical "positive thinkers." They may not be able to tell you why they are happy. They just act happy because someone told them they should.

Although I spent $249 (I sat in the cheap seats), I certainly felt what I got from Tony was worth much more. In fact, this was just the beginning. My next project was to go to Tony's three-and-a-half day *Unleash the Power Within* program. When I checked his program schedule on the internet, at www.tonyrobbins.com, I saw he was scheduled to be in Los Angeles in May. Unfortunately, I was already booked that weekend. Since the church was already reserved (and my fiancée would have killed me), the wedding took precedence, of course. Fortunately, he was scheduled to be in Chicago several months later.

I know you probably think I am crazy for flying to Chicago, spending money on airfare, hotel and $695 for the seminar, just to see Tony live. But it was worth every penny. I have made that money back several times over with the life strategies I learned during those grueling 3 1/2 days.

Our schedule was intense:

Friday....................... 5:30 p.m. – 1:30 a.m.
Saturday................... 9:30 a.m. – 10:00 p.m.
Sunday .... 9:00 a.m. – 12:30 a.m.
Monday.................... 9:00 a.m. – 5:00 p.m.

Can you believe that he packs all that in for $695! It was the best money I ever spent (with the possible exception of the engagement ring I gave my fiancée). *The Unleash the Power Within* seminar was also the last piece necessary to write this comprehensive book about all that Tony has done for my life and what he can do for yours.

The people that attended the seminar were from all walks of life, in different stages of their Tony Robbins experiences. There were many individuals who had never heard of him before and attended the seminar because one of their friends/loved ones gave them a free ticket. I spoke to two ladies who said their boyfriends gave them a free ticket because of what Tony had done for their lives. One lady told me that her boyfriend spent over $23,000 on Tony's worldwide seminars last year alone! I also spoke to other individuals who, like me, had been involved with Tony's books/tapes/seminars for close to a decade. These folks were doing extremely well. You could tell just from a five-minute conversation that they had their act together. Despite their success, they still spent the time and money to come to Chicago to improve their lives even more. I learned that weekend that it's good to surround yourself with people like that. It's hard to not be motivated when you are surrounded by such determined folks.

I used to think that my experience with Tony was unique, but after hearing many other success stories, I believe I'm telling a fairly typical tale. These people went through the same process I did. Our common denominator was that we all decided to improve our lives and chose Tony to guide us.

During the *Unleash the Power Within* seminar, I noticed that others were making dramatic changes in their levels of energy and confidence. They became determined to continue a program of self-improvement. In fact, three of my fellow seatmates chose to enroll in Tony's *Mastery University* – a series of events during the next twelve to eighteen months designed to help them take total control of their lives. It was a major commitment, since they each plunked down $10,000 for the special package Tony offered that night.

The following is an excerpt from my success journal regarding the seminar:

> *It's 6:45 a.m. and I'm on my way to Chicago to see my man Tony Robbins. I am excited to be taking the initiative to go on this journey to* Unleash the Power Within. *I am amazed at myself for spending this much money for personal improvement. I am leaving my comfortable life and beautiful girl for unfamiliar surroundings in an unfamiliar city just because I want to improve myself. Someone who is willing to take that kind of initiative without a guarantee of immediate financial benefit will undoubtedly do well in life. Few people I know will take four full days out of their busy schedules to improve themselves. I will do my best to get as much out of this experience as possible.*
>
> *I feel super focused on my outcomes for the weekend. I believe in what Tony has to say. I have almost written*

an entire book about it. This is a major opportunity. I
remember being on fired up after just a one-day seminar
last year. This seminar is 3 1/2 days and will focus on
improving all categories of my life and breaking through
any fears I still have.

Don't kid yourself, you still have fears. Even Tony
does. I'm doing great and I'm happy with my progress,
but I still have a long way to go. That's okay because the
journey is the most exciting part.

I did the firewalk! What an incredible experience!
Tony uses the firewalk symbolically to show that we can
break through our biggest fears. He first took us outside
the convention center to look at and feel the burning
coals. It was hot just standing next to them. I didn't think
there was a chance in hell I was going to walk across a
bed of coals that were 1600^0 F. It was simply a matter of
being in the right physical state and employing the right
strategy. Most of the attendees walked through "fire"
that night. It was an amazing sight to behold. Although it
was not totally painless for me – I didn't follow the
directions thoroughly and didn't immediately wipe off my
feet – everyone I talked to felt no pain or burning at all.
The main thing we all learned was there is nothing out
there that should scare us away from taking action. If we
can get ourselves to walk barefoot over fiery coals, we
can get ourselves to lose weight, stop smoking, call that
pretty girl/guy, make that sales call, etc.

On my way back to L.A. after a great seminar.
Learned a lot from Tony again. This was the best
learning experience so far. We really immersed ourselves

and stepped up for the entire weekend. The extra long days showed me that it is possible to work super hard and still enjoy the day. The short amount of time I had to relax and have fun was extremely magnified. Having a nice bed-time snack and watching "The X-Files" was serious quality time. I went to bed feeling satisfied. I want to have this feeling every day. Despite the long day, I was not stressed or tired at all.

Just did my first state change (without Tony) by jumping up and down to Britney Spears. What a difference that five minutes made. I went from being half-asleep and needing coffee to feeling totally awake and alive. Ready to kick some serious butt for the day! I must do this every morning. Not just once, but whenever necessary to get into a peak state. I want to live in a peak state every day. Tony does. It feels so much better to live this way than to slug around all morning. I don't need to wait until I go running to feel this great. I can feel great right now – with my pajamas on and the clock still pointing to a very early hour. I can change how I feel in an instant. Don't ever forget this! Last year I did not sustain what I learned from the one-day seminar for more than a month. I did not make this a habit. This time I will. I will live my life as though I am at a Tony Robbins seminar. Full of energy. Full of life. Full of enthusiasm and possibility. I know I'm doing pretty well now, but I just saw what it is like to live in a peak state for three consecutive days. I like that feeling. Let's shoot for this every day. I feel like there is nothing I cannot accomplish in this peak state. Let's do this for the rest of my life. Tony has shown it is possible, having done it for twenty-four years. I heard that his seminars were even longer and more intense several years ago. They used to do this for fourteen to fifteen hours per day for two straight weeks. Wow!

I want to have his energy. I must do what it takes to get to that level. I just need to model his successful strategies. Today, I'm planning to show the world what I have learned. It's time for Manny Ibay to step up and show his full potential. No more crappy days where I do the minimum. I go balls out from now on.

*I decided that next time I face a difficult challenge – a bad call from a client, a letter from an opposing attorney threatening sanctions, etc., – I will first put myself in a peak state before taking on the challenge. Let's start the post-*Unleash the Power Within *weekend with a bang. I will keep the blue bracelet on [that allows us to enter seminar] until I make "Getting in the Proper State" a daily habit.*

Wow! My first full day of work after the seminar was amazing. I don't think I ever worked that hard and maintained such an energetic state for an entire day. Especially without a pressing deadline. I could have decided to do nothing (or very little) yesterday, but I chose to go balls out! I did this without my customary can of Coca-Cola (caffeine). Is it really possible to have that kind of energy every day? I maintained the schedule of the seminar. Every 30-45 minutes (or whenever I noticed that my body wanted to quit on me), I decided to get my body into a peak state. Before going to work I *went to Best Buy and picked up a couple of Dance-mix CD's (*Ultimate Dance Party, *Vols. 1 & 2) in order to re-create the vibrant musical environment Tony provided. What a difference the proper music can make. The mistake I made last year was that I didn't have the proper music on demand. I relied on the radio, which didn't always provide the right song to get me into a peak state. (I'm very selective about what moves me.) Now I'm totally prepared.*

Despite the noise pollution I may have created (I did get permission from my office neighbors first), I was able to create the proper physiology to work at my potential. When I wanted to get a task done, I immediately got into the proper state. What a wonderful feeling it is to know that I now have this ability. You can do it, too.

The best part about yesterday was that I used Tony's strategy to break my negative pattern when I received a bad voice mail. Rather than worry about it, I cranked up my new CD's and made the positive movements we learned to get into the proper state. I used my body to get strong and confident, then dealt with the person who left me the potentially bad message. Thanks, Tony!

Putting Principles Into Practice

You may think this sounds easy, but most of us weren't trained to use our bodies in this fashion. I used to believe that my thoughts created my actions. Now, Tony has taught me the exact opposite. To use my actions (moving my physical body) to shape my thoughts and feelings. You are probably asking yourself, "Why isn't everyone doing this if it's so easy?" Let me tell you a true story Tony told us that illustrates the point that sometimes things really *are* easy, as long as you know what to do.

Everyone has heard of (if not used) Federal Express. When the company first started out, all their deliveries went through a giant structure in Memphis. There was a series of conveyor belts that moved packages throughout the building. If the belts stopped moving, that could cost FEDEX hundreds of thousands of dollars. Fred Smith understood this and took the appropriate precautions by having several back-up systems. However, one day, the belts stopped moving. The back-up systems failed to operate. They tried everything. In a panic, he called the maintenance company and they sent over one of their top guys. After a careful inspection, he turned a particular screw just a little bit. Presto! Everything started working again. Fred was extremely thankful and asked how much. The repairman told him $10,000. Fred was outraged. "All you did was turn a screw. How can you charge me that much? I want an itemized bill." The repairman asked for piece of paper and wrote out his bill. It read:

Turning screw	$1
Knowing what screw to turn	$9,999

Fred Smith gladly paid the bill. It goes to show that "difficult" or seemingly "impossible" things (including peak performance and success) can indeed be easy. You just need to know how to do it. Luckily for me, Tony provided the understanding of what "screws" to turn.

Have I neglected to mention that Tony is quite an entertaining person? Even if you were not interested in anything he had to say, he would have kept you laughing throughout the weekend with his incredible wit and charm. At times, I thought I was there to see Jerry Seinfeld or Chris Rock.

I want to conclude this chapter by discussing how Tony teaches us to help others. One of the most moving talks I ever heard was given by Tony during the *Competitive Edge* seminar. In it, he described how his family was unable to afford a Thanksgiving dinner and how an unknown stranger brought a dinner to their door. Tony says this experience was what caused him to now spend his Thanksgivings feeding thousands of hungry families each year. In his most compassionate and empathetic voice he asked all of us do what we could to help out the less fortunate. He was literally on the verge of tears as he talked to us that night. It was something I will remember forever. Thank you, Tony, for sharing your true self with us that night!

22

---◆---

TONY'S CLARITY
ABOUT THE 9-11 CRISIS

It was a day that none of us will ever forget. Even though I saw the destruction with my own eyes, I could hardly believe it was really happening. The only time I had seen such a disregard for human life was from the super villains in the Superman movies. But there, of course, Superman appeared to save the day. Unfortunately, that was not the case on September 11, 2001.

Prior to that day, things were cruising along quite well for me. In fact, I was scheduled to deliver the first draft of this book to my editor on that very day. My first reaction was to cancel the appointment because it would be too difficult to work under such conditions. However, when I called my editor she suggested that we keep our scheduled meeting. She didn't think we should let those villains mess up our schedules in addition to the damage they had already caused. Fortunately, we did meet that day and I dropped off my manuscript.

The next few weeks were difficult. Although I did manage to get the editorial process underway, I had trouble focusing on any of my major outcomes. I tried many of the strategies I discussed in this book, but couldn't get myself into the proper peak state. In the back of my mind, all I could think about was the damage those suicidal haters had caused. I'm sure most Americans had similar difficulties. In addition, I began to feel fearful about the future, something I hadn't felt in quite some time. It was similar to the feelings I had prior to beginning Tony's program. A sense of helplessness. No real direction. A lack of focus on the tasks at hand. All of a sudden, I didn't feel like the same person who wrote this book. I needed a new strategy to cope with our changed world.

Let me give you an idea of my typical day during this crisis. Earlier you read about the well-organized days that gave me the best chance of peak performance. Unfortunately, those were frightfully interrupted. The positive journal writing and morning exercise sessions were replaced by endless hours watching CNN and MSNBC. I rarely watched the news before this event, since it usually led me to focus on negative things. However, this time I couldn't seem to avoid it. I don't know if it was out of fear or curiosity, but I had to keep watching. Even though they said almost the same thing every hour, I felt I had to be on top of everything that was going on. Instead of focusing on my major goals, such as promoting this book or going to the gym, I became addicted to news programs. The momentum I had built for myself seemed to be dissipating. I didn't feel like I was doing what I wanted when I wanted. I had a trip to Hong Kong scheduled for September 22 but ended up canceling due to my fears. I knew this was not the person who wrote this book about designing your life to do what you want.

Fortunately, Tony was there again to save the day. For some

reason, I knew he would do something to help everyone out. I checked his web site (tonyrobbins.com) for the next couple of days until I found a letter he had published that tried to make some sense of everything and use the current events to strengthen our lives. Soon thereafter, he gave a free web-cast where he spoke about the events of September 11 and how we could get back to normal.

I highly recommend that you visit his web site and listen to what Tony has to say about September 11. Here are some key points he discussed that I wrote in my success journal:

1) *We can actually make our lives as good or better if we take conscious control over our decisions.*

2) *People who have faced death/loss of freedom really know what living is all about.*

3) *When you start to take action the anger/depression disappears. It can be action to help the victims of the tragedy or toward your own personal goals.*

4) *The emotion of the event must move you into action. If you get stuck in anger/depression you cannot be of help to anyone.*

5) *We must start directing our own focus instead of allowing the media to control it.*

6) *If you focus only on all of humanity's pain you couldn't live. There are people dying of starvation and acts of terrorism daily. But there are a lot of great things happening every day as well. Choose to focus on these things and be empowered.*

7) *The key to leadership is to find an empowering meaning for the crisis and use it to motivate yourself and others.*

8) *Don't reward the villains by allowing their acts to ruin your life. Defy them by living your life at an even higher level.*

9) *You must incorporate in your own personal life the meaning the events of 9-11 has for you. Find a way to use the event for greater good, e.g.,*
   - *God is challenging me.*
   - *This makes me appreciate life more.*
   - *I will now appreciate the freedom this country has to offer – something I formerly took for granted.*
   - *I will live at a higher level to defy the villains and show them that they can't harm me.*

10) *Although they are just doing their jobs, the media is getting us to focus on what we fear and what we have no control over.*

11) *Getting on a plane was always a risk in the past. You knew that there was a slight chance something could go wrong. However, you decided to accept that risk because the opportunity to travel far outweighed that risk. Remember, there are 8.8 million flights per year. You are still safer in the air than driving on the freeway.*

12) *The challenge for us is to become more. Every generation has had to face some type of major adversity, e.g., the Great Depression, World War II. History also shows us that following these events we have seen the best times in American history. These challenges present an opportunity to cleanse ourselves and move to a new level.*

13) *The ultimate antidote for fear is gratitude.*

14) *The message of 9-11 should be to live fully today. Face death and decide to live.*

Re-Taking Control of My Life

Now this way of thinking was not totally new to an avid follower like me. However, Tony offered a different spin, one I needed to hear. Although I had already used these techniques, it was helpful to hear them applied to our nation's recent tragedy. The first step I took was to limit my news watching. As Tony says, the media makes us focus on things we fear and have no control over. No one likes the feeling of helplessness. Yes, I did still watch the news, but just to get the main headlines. It didn't require a major portion of my day.

The next thing I did was to get back to doing what I wanted to do. As I mentioned earlier, I love traveling. Rather than sitting at home and worrying about going anywhere, I decided to face down my fears. On the night before my first post 9-11 airline trip I didn't sleep very well. (Normally, I sleep like a baby.) However, once we got on the plane, those fears dissipated. After a couple of flights, I was almost back to normal. Yes, there might have been a touch of apprehension, but nothing that could keep me from going where I wanted to go. If you have stopped traveling I highly recommend that you get back on a plane before you psyche yourself out of flying forever.

Despite all the good things happening in my life, I still needed my "success coach" to help me make periodic adjustments in my daily thinking. The next couple of months actually turned out to be some of my most fruitful ever. Using Tony's advice, I traveled to Washington, D.C.; Paris; Switzerland; Hong Kong; the Philippines; New York and Maui within four months. I needed to prove to myself that I controlled my destiny. It was not subject to the whims of someone who hides in a cave. Here are some journal entries from my trip to Europe that show how I personally adapted to 9/11:

Bonjour! It is amazing to be back in Paris for a third time. This place is always exciting. The best part about this trip is that it is not only a vacation but a chance to exorcise my fears about traveling. We decided to continue living our lives and focus on what we wanted to do, instead of reacting in fear about what is happening. As long as we play it smart we should be fine. It is much less scary when you are actually doing something, e.g., traveling/flying instead of thinking and worrying about it.

Tony's letter and webcast, along with my own struggles during the past ten years, have certainly helped me cope with this crisis.

We just came back from an amazing run through the streets of Paris. We ran from the Tuileries Garden over a bridge with a fantastic view of the Seine, and finished by circling the Louvre.

Hello from Switzerland! Just came back from our second run in Zurich. It is great that we continued our physical fitness program even while we are on vacation. Remember, it is an even greater accomplishment to work out on vacation not only because you are out of your element but also because you have been indulging in great food and wine every night (allowed only on vacation!). Yesterday we got a great look at the Swiss Alps – 10,000 feet up!

During my run today, I realized that the most important thing I can learn from 9-11 and Tony is that we really need to focus on what we want – our outcomes. We can't waste time and energy focusing on all the negative things going on out there. Prior to 9-11 I was excellent at focusing on all the great things in my life and the world. However, the time I wasted in front of the television set watching the news over and over isn't going to help my future or anyone else's. All we can do is contribute as much as we can to those who need help and focus on what is required to reach our objectives. I need to get back to that on a daily basis. No point in wasting my time on things I can't control.

The best thing I can do for my country and myself is to remain as productive as possible to help boost our nation's economy. If everyone followed this course of action, we would recover quickly from this temporary recession.

This experience reminded me that I need to continually keep learning and improving. Unexpected events can slow down your momentum, but with the proper desire to adapt, you can quickly get back on track. Thanks again, Tony, for your response to 9-11 and being our "Superman."

23

$\blacklozenge$

MY EMOTIONAL
FLOOD – ACCENTUATING
THE POSITIVE

One reason Tony Robbins has become an international success is his ability to make us feel good about ourselves. In *The Time of Your Life*, he introduces the concept of an "emotional flood." This is designed precisely for those moments when you need to fight against a major setback. When I lose a big trial or a major business deal, I turn to Tony's emotional flood to get me back on track. The tendency after a project has gone bad is to go over it many times in your head. Although it is good to learn from your mistakes, you must know when to forget about them and move on.

Tony taught me that the best way to move on is to "flood" my thoughts with positive and fun memories. My usual routine is to think about all the victories I have enjoyed in the past. If I just lost a big case, I will try to recall the trials I previously won. I then focus on all the happiest times of my life, in particular the victories and vacations I have experienced. This is where a success journal really helps. I can turn directly to a day where I won my last case and see how I felt. Here are some excerpts

from my success journal that I use & re-use to get a positive
feeling back:

*I just finished arguing the GG appeal. I think we won!
Although it is not yet official, I believe the judges will
give my client his day in court. I worked really hard to
get ready and spent over seventy-five hours writing it. I
WAS READY! This is what I have been working toward
for the past six years by focusing on one thing. This feels
great. My client was in tears he was so excited. Keep up
the hard work and more good things will happen.*

*(Two weeks later) I won my appeal! Party time! We
will go back to the trial court to decide this case. This is
very exciting. I have been working hard since getting this
new office and the cash will start tumbling in. I am very
excited. Tonight, I'll be seeing my mentor Dale and look
forward to being inspired to get to the next level. This is
a great feeling. I feel like I have the golden touch. I am
winning the cases I need to win to further my
career/business. Keep trying to improve your skills and
the sky is the limit. You will be The Man, Master of the
Universe, if you continue to try to improve daily. Just
keep doing what you know you should keep doing. You
are on your way!*

*We won $80,000! (That was after they offered us only
$7,500 before trial.) I am thrilled with the effort and
determination I put into the case. I think my hard work is
starting to pay off. I must use this experience to get to the*

next level. I beat someone who has much more trial experience than I do. The jury liked me a lot. I am an extremely convincing and entertaining person! All those years selling LDS & ARS paid off. If I can sell that kind of BS, I definitely can sell myself and my client. I am coming into my own. I am developing into someone I can very proud of. I must continue to improve by taking seminars on trial practice. Dale says that I must always keep learning. Even though he has accomplished so much, he still says that he learns something every day about being a lawyer. I will use this victory to give me the toughness to settle/try my other cases and kick some butt!

(The next day) I am still beaming from our victory. The congratulations are coming in. My parents were very happy to hear about it on their vacation in the Philippines. Finally, I must be looking damn good. Use this energy to take yourself to the next level. This is the life. I am at home at 10 a.m. on a weekday, after a great run with my girl, planning my day. I am living the life I always dreamed of – working hard at something I am excited and proud about (being a trial lawyer), winning trials with my own business. That is the ultimate. I know that I control my destiny! I have designed my life to be just where it is right now. No one tells me when to go to work or how hard to work. I decide for myself.

Furthermore, I can re-live some of my favorite days on vacation. I always make it a point while I am on a trip to capture exactly what I am thinking and feeling at the time. It really adds to my emotional flood and gives an excellent perspective of what I have accomplished. My self-worth no longer consists of the trial I may have just lost, it also includes these recent experiences I have enjoyed. Here are some of my favorites:

Our second day in Paris. Had a very good time in London. Learned a lot about life and the struggle that some people have just to survive. It made me realize that it is very energizing and uplifting to wake up every day knowing I have the opportunity to make it big. We live in a great country. I am not constrained by anything and don't have to do anything I don't want. Must use this learning experience anytime I think I don't have it great. Additionally, I must use this experience always to tell myself to strive to grow and expand, especially if I have the opportunity.

Read Tony Robbins at Les Deux Magots, the same place where Jean Paul Sartre wrote. I'd love to write in Paris someday myself. Belief in what I can do is the key. I wouldn't be here in Paris, only 3 months after I was in Maui, if I didn't believe it could be done. Most people think you can only take one of these trips in an entire year. I plan to travel at least 4 times per year because I believe I can do so, while at the same time expanding my business & saving the money I need to reach my other goals.

Our 3rd day in Florence. We went to the Rossi Villa (of Martini & Rossi) for a great hike, wine/olive oil tasting and an authentic pasta lunch in the small town of Villa Magna. I bought the leather jacket I have wanted for a long time. It seems amazing to think that we are here in Florence, halfway around the world. It does not seem real. But it is. We are especially thankful that we can be here, considering that most people will never get to see this place.

This view of St. Thomas is what it is all about. This has to be one of the most amazing views I have ever seen. Green mountains dotted with big houses. Bright red roofs. Blue-green clear water with many sailboats docked. An amazing coastline. All from my first class verandah suite. This rocks! We just came back from the beach in St. John – Trunks Bay. That was amazing. I was in the water looking out at the scenery, thinking about how I was looking forward to this during the GG trial. I kicked butt on the trial and with excellent planning turned this week into a trip of a lifetime. [That was the cruise ship proposal vacation.]

By the way, as I'm copying this from my success journal I am getting a major Emotional Flood!

Our last full day on the cruise…just came back from Half Moon Cay in the Bahamas – Paradise! The most amazing beach with crystal clear water. It was nice to lie in the hammock looking out at our cruise ship docked in the middle of the ocean. This is the way to go – we will definitely be going on more spectacular vacations from now on. Work hard/play hard! I worked super hard from January to May just as I said I would. And now I am enjoying the Great Life!

I am looking at Holland America's private island which, we have just come from, sitting on my private verandah sipping a tropical beverage. Does it get any better than this? This rocks! I love it when a plan comes together (The A-Team)! I have come a long way since my days at LDS and ARS. Back then I hated what I was doing, dreading each work day and making little money – which meant I couldn't have a lot of fun. Now I'm doing something every day that I am super excited about – I look forward to each day equally and make pretty good money. Enough to do the things I want to do. No one tells me what to do except me! That is what everybody is shooting for!

Wow! I am feeling great. We're not done yet. Tony then asks us to visualize what our future will look like after achieving our big dreams. I've done this exercise many times in my journal. This is one of my favorites:

I'm sitting on the second-floor terrace of our Bel Air estate enjoying the warm morning air, looking at a beautiful view of the Century City skyline. The cell phone rings and it's my client, thanking me again for winning his multi-million dollar lawsuit against a Fortune 500 company. My wife comes over to join me and we start talking about our trip to Paris. Tomorrow we are going on our annual family trip to Europe. We have a beautiful apartment overlooking the Champs Elysées where we will spend the next month sampling the fine cuisine and wines the city has to offer. Since I've become fluent in French, it will be just like home.

My good friends Denis and John have just arrived. They are here to pick up my Ferrari 360 Spyder that they will baby-sit for the next month. I remember how they really enjoyed babysitting the Mercedes S500 last year. My son, Austin, comes in very excited since he just broke par for the first time at the Riviera Country Club. Not bad for a twelve-year old. Watch out Tiger! My daughter, Kirin, on the other hand, just won the junior tennis tournament at the club. She wants to be the next Anna Kournikova – tennis player/model.

The phone rings again and it's my parents. They just came back from their daily three mile walk/run and want to coordinate our travel plans. They will be embarking on a round-the-world trip and plan to join us in Paris for a week. I'm excited to spend more quality time with them.

Everyone leaves momentarily and I'm alone on the terrace with my thoughts. I can't believe how great life has turned out, remembering where I was twenty years ago. I think I'll call my good friend Tony Robbins and thank him again for all he has done...

Now I'm really feeling great! This stuff truly works. The problem is, most people don't consciously try to focus on all the great things that have happened (or will happen) in their lives. Use this exercise whenever you are feeling really down on yourself. If you find that your morning power questions are not enough, do an emotional flood!

24

---◆---

MAKING
RELATIONSHIPS WORK

In Tony's books and audio programs he stresses the importance of having quality relationships. He emphasizes that we cannot have "total success" unless we have great relationships with family, friends and business associates. Here are some key points that I wrote in my success journal:

1) *You must know the values and rules of the person whom you share a relationship with.*
2) *A relationship is a place to give, not to take.*
3) *Identify the warning signs early and take tackle the problem immediately.*
4) *Make your relationship one of the highest priorities in your life.*
5) *Focus each day on making it better.*
6) *Never threaten the relationship.*
7) *Re-associate what you love about this person, i.e., ask what is great about this person, keep finding new ways to surprise each other.*

Tony's mission is to teach you what he has learned from the experts. When discussing relationships, he provides information from Barbara DeAnglis, author of the best-selling book, *How to Make Love All the Time*. What I learned from Tony is that you need to model those who are successful in a given area and apply it to your own situation.

For a certain period in my life, I was cynical about the institution of marriage. I did not believe it was something that could really work for me, given my previous history. Even when I did meet my future wife, it took me a while to get out my "single guy" mind-set. As Tony says, it's all about your belief system. It was only when I changed my beliefs that I was able to see the benefits of a quality relationship.

I did not have to look far to see a beautiful long-term relationship. My parents, who have been together for thirty-nine years, have always been extremely happy together. In fact, I don't think I have ever seen them arguing or even raising their voices to one another. From what I observed through the years, they really adhered to Tony's key points about relationships. They obviously considered their relationship their highest priority, far above anything else. I never saw work or friends come between them.

If you have managed to find your ideal mate, you are probably following most of the points Tony has discussed. From a success perspective, having a happy relationship can do wonders for your productivity. I can't begin to tell you how easy everything else seems to be when you have a loving partner to come home to every day. Having a good primary relationship allows you to focus on your goals in life. One friend of mine spent so much of his energy on the problems he was having with his wife that he had little left to focus on what he really wanted. I can remember days when he spent all his time worrying about what she was doing, distracted from the work at hand. I expect most of us have had moments like this in our lives.

I'm not suggesting that you should bolt whenever there are problems. I am a big believer in doing everything possible to save a marriage. You simply need to determine as soon as possible when something just isn't going to work out. If you are unhappy 90 percent of the time, this is a strong indication that this person is not right for you. On the other hand, if you are happy 80 percent of the time but have trouble with the other 20 percent it may be fruitful to try to work things out.

I have some good friends who were having problems in that 20 percent time frame. Their main problem areas involved things that were identifiable and fixable: taking care of their baby, an interfering mother in law and certain spending decisions. But they truly seemed to enjoy spending time together when these "problems" did not get in the way. For instance, they always enjoyed themselves on their trips to Hawaii, where they were away from their everyday problems. I could tell that there was still electricity between them. It was only when life's daily routine got in the way that problems arose. Using the principles Tony discusses could be truly helpful in reminding them of their real love for each other.

Fortunately, I am now in a relationship that maximizes my chances of success. Home is a place where I can relax, recharge and have fun. It is a place I always look forward to returning to after a hard day's work.

———————◆———————

Doing The Maximum

Here is a tip that is guaranteed to take your relationship to its highest level ever: Do the maximum for your spouse/significant other. Make yourself the best husband or wife, boyfriend or girlfriend that you can possibly be. Many people try to do the minimum to get by in a relationship. For instance, I once heard a friend say that he didn't think it was a good idea to go all out for his wife because it would be difficult to maintain such a high level of "niceness." This is the biggest mistake you can make. Instead of asking, "What is the least I can do to get by in this relationship?" you should be asking, "What can I do so that my spouse thinks I am the best husband in the entire world?" Trust me, having a happy partner makes everything else so much easier.

25

♦

TASTING
THE DIFFERENCE

Once we've experienced some degree of success, we tend to forget how far we have actually come. Many things that used to be exciting gradually become part of our routine. Tony has stressed that the key to happiness is to live with an attitude of gratitude. Gratitude especially for all the people, things, and opportunities that you have in your life. As we get caught up in achieving bigger and better things, we often fail to fully appreciate the pleasures we now take for granted.

I recently had an experience that illustrates this. When I first bought my BMW, I was excited just to cruise around, even if I didn't have any particular place to go. However, after a while, driving the BMW became second nature and I forgot about thrill it originally gave me. One day it needed some repairs and I left it with the shop. The manager was nice enough to give me a loaner car so I wouldn't have to spend money on a rental. The car was a Hyundai and it just didn't have the same appeal. In fact, it reminded me of the 1983 Volkswagon I drove when I was making $1,000 per month. Now you just can't look at a girl in the car next to you when you're driving a Hyundai. Since the shop didn't have the necessary part for my BMW, I ended up driving this car for a whole week. It turned out to be a great experience, after all. During the entire time I had the loaner car, I kept thinking how great my BMW was and how eager I was to get it back. Yet two weeks earlier, I hadn't given my car a second thought.

Revisiting Old Times

Just for fun, I started to go back and do some of the things I did when I was making $1,000 per month. I went to the same inexpensive restaurants, played video games – a major source of fun when I had only $2.00 for entertainment and went to bargain matinees. Hey, these things were still fun!

And I didn't stop there. I wanted to really taste what my life was like ten years ago. I parked outside the 450-square-foot single apartment I used to live in and recalled how it felt living there with three dogs. I remembered how I used to look out my window, which faced some elegant townhouses, thinking I could never afford them. I visited one of my old job sites and sat for a while in the parking lot. I peeked into the window of a building where I used to work as a telemarketer for eight hours per day at $8/hour. I almost got a tear in my eye when I realized how far I have come in a short time. I remember thanking Tony Robbins out loud in the car for helping me. Amazing how this week with the Hyundai opened my eyes to all that I have become and made me appreciate all the opportunities I now have.

If you sometimes feel like you are taking your successes for granted, take a trip down memory lane. Do the things you used to do when you were struggling. You'll be surprised how much you appreciate your life as you *taste the difference!*

26

◆

A DECADE WITH TONY

It's hard to believe I've been using the principles taught by Tony Robbins for a decade. Those early days of struggling seem to be a distant memory. As Tony says, "People overestimate what they can do in a year and underestimate what they can do in a decade." I can vouch for that.

The best thing Tony has done is to guide me to take control of my own destiny. Remember, *if you don't control your own destiny, someone else will*! I'm equally excited about each day. I'm just as excited about Monday as I am about Saturday. Life is too short to be doing something you're not excited about.

If you get that sick feeling in your stomach at around 6 or 7 p.m. Sunday night, thinking about going to work the next day, you're not living your dream life. I was the same way ten years ago. Don't fall into the trap that Tony frequently talks about – "Most people get so caught up in making a living that they are unable to design the type of life that they really want."

I have learned that everyone needs a coach, even Tiger Woods and Michael Jordan. Try to get someone like Tony as your coach. And don't be afraid to keep going back to him.

Where Do I Go From Here?

My goal is to continue with Tony's programs for the *next* decade and accomplish the following before my next book:

1) Attend Tony's *Date with Destiny* seminar.
2) Live in Paris, Tuscany and Maui for one month at a time.
3) Increase my income while spending less time at the office.
4) Go on a round-the-world trip – or what I am now calling the *trip of a lifetime.*
5) Help others begin their own success programs to reach their Big Dreams.
6) Increase the quality of my relationships with my wife, family and friends.
7) Get my parents in top physical shape so we can enjoy many quality years together.

I hope that through this book you have grasped the importance of following some type of success program, whether it be from Tony Robbins or one of the other highly qualified success coaches out there.

I also hope that reading my book has given Tony pleasure. I would like to say farewell by telling you my ultimate goal, one that is now in your hands. That would be for one of my readers to take the information he or she has acquired from this book and apply it to create his/her Dream Life. And then of course, to tell the world all about it in a book called *Thank You, Tony Robbins, Too!*

BEST WISHES FOR YOUR DREAM LIFE!